MAKING JESUS LORD

MAKING JESUS LORD

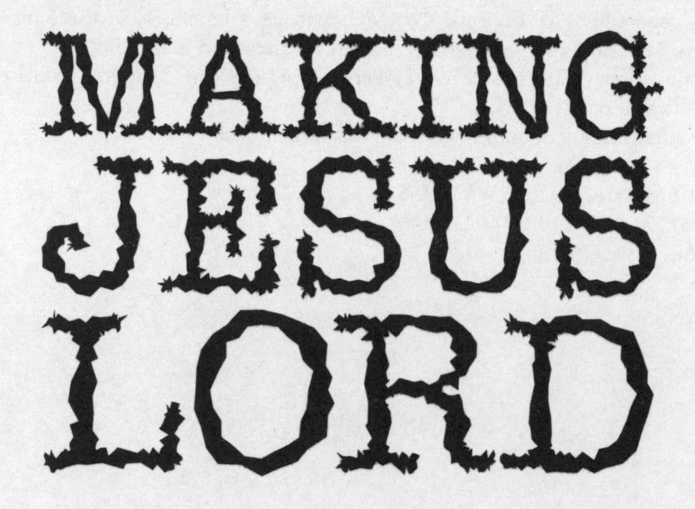

The Dynamic Power of Laying Down Your Rights

LOREN CUNNINGHAM

with Janice Rogers

YWAM PUBLISHING
A Ministry Of Youth With A Mission
P.O. Box 55787, Seattle, WA 98155

YWAM Publishing is the publishing ministry of Youth With A Mission. Youth With A Mission (YWAM) is an international missionary organization of Christians from many denominations dedicated to presenting Jesus Christ to this generation. To this end, YWAM has focused its efforts in three main areas: 1) Training and equipping believers for their part in fulfilling the Great Commission (Matthew 28:19). 2) Personal evangelism. 3) Mercy ministry (medical and relief work).
For a free catalog of books and materials write or call:
YWAM Publishing
P.O. Box 55787, Seattle, WA 98155
(425) 771-1153 or (800) 922-2143
www.ywampublishing.com

Making Jesus Lord
Formerly titled *Winning God's Way*

10 09 08 07 06 05 04 03 02   10 9 8

Published by YWAM Publishing
P.O. Box 55787, Seattle, WA 98155, USA

Verses marked KJV are taken from the King James Version of the Bible.

ISBN 1-57658-012-1

Printed in the United States of America

This book is dedicated to our parents,
Tom and Jewell Cunningham,
who lived out the message of this book on a daily basis.
We not only honor them, but we love them dearly.

Contents

Acknowledgments

Though the content of this book is my own, the skill of writing is that of my sister, Janice. We enjoyed working together as a team, as we did in our previous book *Is That Really You, God?*

We want to thank the individuals who helped us with this book: Rune Aasen, Dr. David Barrett, Andy Beach, Bruce Brander, Harry Conn, Robert Cunningham, T.C Cunningham, Joy Dawson, Terri Genin, David Hazard, Alison Muesing, Kris Pemberton, Brenda Poklacki, Leonard Ravenhill, Dorothea Schmidt, Robert Smith, Ron Smith, Chappell Temple, Keith Warrington, Gerhard Wessler and Thomas Young.

We are especially grateful to our spouses, Darlene and Jimmy, for much help and encouragement; and to our children Karen and David, and Jeffrey, Joel and Jonathan, who wait patiently till the storm of another book is over.

And most of all, we thank you, Lord, for giving up Your rights and coming to earth for us all.

CHAPTER ONE

The Road to the Whole World

It's amazing how one small turn can change your life forever. The last thing I remembered was glancing sleepily at my wife, Darlene, who was driving our Volkswagen van. We were driving home to California from one of the toughest encounters I'd had in my life. I'd driven all night and, around 6 A.M., given the wheel to Darlene. Now, warm dry air from the Arizona highway and surrounding desert blew in through the front window, making her fair complexion flush a little and blowing her short, blonde hair.

I took off my shoes and crawled into a sleeping bag in the back, closing my eyes. *What a treasure she is, Lord,* I thought, my head rocking drowsily with the rhythm of the van. *Especially with all we've just been through....*

The last few weeks had wrung everything out of me. We'd just come from a meeting with the head of our denomination. Because of my choice to start an interdenominational mission, I chose to give up my ministerial status with the church. It was a tough choice, because many of my friends didn't understand my decision.

There was something else, too. A short time before, I had turned down my aunt's offer to join her in a multimillion dollar business. That, too, would have conflicted with what God was telling me to do, and I wanted to obey Him at all cost.

So I had burned all my bridges behind me. Darlene had touched my heart, standing steadfastly at my side as I'd laid down both my chance for a bright financial future and the prospects of a successful career in the church. I'd given up everything to follow the Lord's call to pioneer an international mission. It was just Darlene and me now. There was almost nothing left to give up.

...I startled from sleep, to find myself rolling around violently inside the van, tossed like a wad of paper. With a sickening crunch of metal and glass, the van was rolling, from its side to its top, to its other side down the highway while my head and body slammed painfully against the inside walls.

Suddenly, I was flung out a side window as far as my waist. The pavement came rushing up at my face, while the van continued to roll on top of me. Knowing I'd be crushed, I slapped my hands against the pavement and pushed myself back inside.

Then everything went black.

I must have regained consciousness only seconds later, for I was outside the van and clouds of dust were just settling around me, revealing the bleakest, most barren desert I had ever seen. Not a house or tree in sight. Struggling, I sat up in a daze. Nothing looked familiar. Something warm and wet began running down my head.

I reached up to wipe it away, and my fingers came down covered with blood. My head ached, and I couldn't make sense of what I was doing sitting in this wreckage.

To my left lay the crushed heap that was our van.

Scattered around me were all the things we owned—suitcases were strewn about, some broken open, with shirts, underwear and socks laying in the dirt.

For one frozen minute I tried to think. *What had happened?* I remembered the difficult meeting...driving through the night...climbing in back to sleep...Darlene was driving when....

My heart lurched.

Frantically, I scrambled to my knees. Where was Darlene?

Then I saw her—unmoving. She lay face down under a heavy suitcase a few yards away.

"Darlene!" I screamed her name, crawling towards her. There was a brick in my stomach. Lifting the suitcase off of her, I saw that a gash had opened her head in back. Gently, I turned her over. She was not breathing. Her eyes were wide open. Unseeing. Fixed.

Cradling her bruised, bloody head in my lap, I rocked her. *She's gone!* Tears ran down my cheeks. I thought I had lost so much when I gave up my aunt's business offer and my ministerial credentials. But now, in a moment's time everything was lost—our van was totaled, our belongings were scattered in the dust of the desert, and the one person who mattered most to me was dead.

I looked around wildly at the wreckage. It seemed to symbolize our life. All was gone. Gusts of wind blew stinging needles of sand in my face.

What happened next on that desolate stretch of desert road defies all reason. There, with not a living thing around me for miles, a voice spoke my name aloud.

"Loren!"

I looked around. Then I knew. Even though I had never heard His voice with my ears before, I recognized it as the voice of God.

"Yes, Lord?" I responded, my voice choked with emotion.

"Loren, will you still serve me?"

Why did He have to ask me? There was nothing else left in my life now but Him.

Through tears I looked into the clear desert sky and answered. "Yes, Lord, I'll serve you. I have nothing left except my life...and you can have that, too."

In a moment, the Lord spoke a second time.

"Pray for Darlene."

Until I heard those words, I hadn't even thought of praying. I thought she was dead. But I began to pray with all my might.

To my astonishment, she drew a rattly-sounding breath. She was fighting to breathe, still unconscious.

Other things began to happen.

A Mexican man came by in a pickup and went for help. In a little over an hour, we were in an ambulance, headed for the nearest hospital, more than ninety miles away. As we drove, the ambulance screaming down the highway at almost a hundred miles an hour, our circumstances became clear to me. Darlene had mistakenly turned off the main highway, and our accident had taken place on a small road a few miles from the Mexican border.

As I sat beside Darlene in the ambulance, God spoke to me for the third time, this time inside my mind. He said that Darlene was going to be okay. As soon as those words flashed into my mind, she opened her eyes, rolled her head slightly on the gurney and smiled at me. Later, she wouldn't be able to remember doing that.

When we arrived at the hospital, Darlene and I were rushed into the emergency room. My injuries were cared for at once—they wrapped my head in bandages and prescribed a back brace. We were separated in the emergency room by curtains, but I heard Darlene when she regained consciousness. She began calling my name frantically.

"I'm here, honey. It's all right," I called to her through the curtains. She must have feared I was dead.

Darlene had an injured back and head injuries. My back was hurt and I was badly bruised. But we would mend. It was several days before Darlene was released from the hospital, but I left the same day—walking stiffly, clad in the same bloodstained clothes and without any shoes on. My shoes and our other possessions were waiting beside our wrecked van.

Later, there was astounding news. Darlene and I found out that at the same hour as our accident, a group of ladies were gathered in a Los Angeles suburb for their Thursday morning prayer meeting. One woman who knew of us and our work had told the group she believed they were to pray for Loren and Darlene Cunningham. They started to intercede. That same morning, in northern California, a friend named Berniece Coff Siegel felt she was not to eat lunch, but to spend the time praying for us instead.

I suppose some may say that I didn't really hear the audible voice of God that day in the desert. I was in quite an emotional state at the time, and I can't really prove it. I have heard God speak in my mind many times, guiding me, but I believe that day was different. But then, as I have reflected on this experience, I've come to realize that it was not primarily a lesson in how God speaks to His children.

What was burned into my heart that day was a lesson on the power that God can release when we lay down our rights. Until the moment I thought I'd lost everything, I never realized that nothing in this life actually belongs to me. I would speak of *my* car, *my* wife, *my* ministry. After the accident, I realized for the first time how easily I could lose it all in seconds.

Everything we have is given to us by God for a time, to use for His glory. These new thoughts started me on a quest through scripture to learn what God had to say on this important subject. What began as a Bible survey became far more than that. The insight I gained transformed me, becoming a keystone of my life and of the missionary organization that was birthed, Youth With A Mission. In short, I found through the Bible—especially in the life of Jesus—that the way to win is to give up!

Not that we give up in our struggle with evil. On the contrary. In more than twenty-five years of international ministry, I have learned through some dramatic circumstances that laying down my rights is a key to winning major battles with the formidable forces of Satan.

When we surrender our personal rights to the Lord, for His sake and the sake of the gospel, we discover the secret of inheriting the whole world for Him.

For the Christian there can be no more important and exciting subject to explore.

CHAPTER TWO

Walking Barefoot

I have lived in Hawaii on the campus of YWAM's Pacific and Asia Christian University for the last ten years and we go barefoot a lot. I love to come home and kick off my shoes at the door. It's very common here to follow the Asian custom of taking your shoes off when you enter a home.

In scripture, taking your shoes off had a very special meaning. When Moses had his first confrontation with God at the burning bush, God told him to take off his shoes because he was standing on holy ground.

Boaz's relative took his shoe off while negotiating with him over the right to marry Ruth.

David, after being defeated in rebellion, left Jerusalem walking barefoot.

Jesus walked barefoot to Calvary.

What was the significance? In the culture of that time, being unshod was the sign that you were a slave. Moses knew exactly what was meant when God told him to take off his shoes. He had grown up in Pharaoh's palace where there were lots of slaves. A slave had no rights. A slave didn't wear shoes. In the burning presence of God, Moses was asked to give up his rights, become God's servant and accept the assignment God was giving him to go and deliver His people.

David's humiliation as a conquered king was shown by his walking barefoot out of the city. Boaz's kinsman removed his shoe to close the contract over Ruth, and by so doing was swearing on his right to remain a free man.

Jesus gave us the supreme example of giving up everything for a greater goal. It says in Philippians 2 that He did not count equality with God a thing to be grasped but emptied Himself, taking the form of a bond-servant—a slave. Slaves have no rights, and Jesus became a slave for our sakes.

Look at the rights Jesus freely surrendered. First of all, the right to be God—He gave that up to come to earth as a man. We cannot fathom what it was like for the Son of God to leave Heaven and come into our sinful world.

On this planet, He gave up the rights to a normal birth. We may glamorize the circumstances in Christmas celebrations, but anyone who has been in an Asian stable knows it is damp, drafty and reeks of animal dung.

He gave up the rights to be with His earthly family. He left His widowed mother behind to travel in His ministry.

He gave up the right to marriage and the right to a home, saying that even the birds of the air had their nests and the foxes had their dens, but He didn't have a place to lay His head.

He gave up the right to money. He once had to borrow a coin from someone for a sermon illustration!

He surrendered His reputation. As far as most people were concerned, He was an illegitimate son, raised in a town that was scorned. The ultimate slur to His reputation came when He, the Son of God, was called a devil by the religious experts of His time. Think of what that must have meant in His spirit!

But He went even further. Jesus gave up the right to life itself and became obedient to death on a cross. Not just a normal death, but the death reserved for the worst criminals of His day. He was buried in a borrowed tomb, then He tore away His very last right by descending to the depths of Hell itself.

Why did He do all this? First, that He might restore us to God. No wonder the Father promised to exalt Him and give Him a name above every other name, that at Jesus' name every knee should bow! But there's another reason. Jesus was showing us how to live our lives. He was showing us how to win over the devil. He was giving us the strategy for accomplishing the greatest job ever given to man—taking over the earth from Satan and winning it back for God. Jesus was showing us that the only way to conquer is to submit.

Jesus wants us to follow Him, going barefoot, losing our rights and gaining the world. Only by taking Jesus' example into every part of our lives will we be able to win in life, ruling and reigning with Him.

He spelled it out for us in Mark 8:34,35:

"If any man would come after me, let him deny himself and take up his cross and follow me. For whoever would save his life will lose it; and whoever loses his life for my sake and the gospel's will save it."

This is how it works. First, God gives you rights. It says in the Bible that every good and perfect gift comes down from the Father (James 1:17). God gave you the right to a family. God gave you the right to have things, the right to freedom, the right to your country, and many other basic blessings. They are good. We are not following God's truth if we say, like the Hindus, that the material world is evil. Or if we teach, like the Buddhists, that only in turning away from the things of this world will we achieve reality. No. God looked at the earth He created and said "It is good."

And God looks at you and what He has given you and says, "It is good."

Then why is He asking us to give Him back those rights? Because it is really the only way we can express our love back to Him.

When my children were little, they came and asked me for money which they took to the store to buy a present for my birthday. The fact was, I was actually paying for my own gift. But that was not the point. I gave to them so they could turn around and show their love by giving back to me.

It is the same with our heavenly Father. We have nothing that He hasn't given us. When we give freely to Him, it is because we want to show Him our love. God owns all the earth, all the universe, but when we give Him what He has blessed us with, the expression of our love brings joy to His father heart.

Another reason God asks for us to relinquish something is because He wants to give us something greater. It is a rule of the Kingdom of God: Give up something good and receive something of greater value; give up your rights and receive greater privileges with God.

Jacob wrestled with God, was wounded in his hip, and became a Prince, a leader of a nation. But he limped for the rest of his life. Every strong man or woman of God has gone this route. The choice is yours: Remain in mediocrity and miss out on God's greater purposes for you, or walk with a limp and be a prince.

God promised Joshua, "Every place that the sole of your foot will tread upon I have given to you..." (Joshua 1:3). God didn't say the sole of his *shoe,* but the sole of his *foot.* Being barefoot is the sign of humility, of having given up all. To the barefoot, God promises possession of the nations, to rule and reign with Jesus, the returning King of kings and Lord of lords.

He is promising us the greatest privilege of all: winning this world for the Kingdom of God.

CHAPTER THREE

Every Good and Perfect Gift

One of the most precious gifts God gives us is the right to be part of a family. God's will is for every baby born on earth to have a loving father and mother who will nurture him or her to full potential as a unique creation of the heavenly Father. That's God's will.

It is His will that each one of us draw security, love and a sense of who we are from our living family and even from those who have gone before. He wants us to know our roots. I believe that is one reason He devoted so much space in the Bible to genealogies. Those long lists show us that He doesn't want us to reject our heritage. It is a good thing to find out about our ancestors and thank Him for whatever good we have derived from them.

Further, it is God's will that a man and woman should come together in a loving triangle with Him at the head, reflecting His love and unity in marriage. This is a gift of

God, first given in the Garden of Eden when the Lord said it wasn't good for man to be alone.

A child is a gift of God to his parents, a delight in their youth and a help in their old age. God gives parents the right and privilege of raising godly offspring.

Marriage and family were the cornerstones God laid for a secure society of individuals. He intends the family to be a bulwark against all the evil influences of Satan in this world—a protection against the assaults on the human spirit that we face because of our sin-filled world.

Family and home are all of this and more. They are good and perfect gifts, coming down from the Father. Yet they are also gifts that He requires us to hold lightly, never putting them before Him and His work. We often think of idolatry in terms of heathen lands and carved images. But idolatry is merely loving and serving anything more than God. Your wife, your husband, your children or your parents could be an idol in your heart.

You may ask, "Doesn't 1 Timothy 5:8 say a man who doesn't take care of his family is worse than an infidel?" Yes, definitely. We are never to give up responsibility for our family. God would not require a man to abandon wife and children for the sake of the gospel. Neither is it His will for us to shrug off our responsibilities for elderly parents. He pointed out the blatant selfishness of the Pharisees who absolved themselves of parental support while "doing God's work" (Mark 7:11).

You can almost write it out, like a mathematical equation:

RESPONSIBILITIES – RIGHTS =
REWARDS OF RELATIONSHIP WITH GOD

While He never requires us to be irresponsible concerning our families, God does ask us to place our love for family and our desire to be with them on the altar. Love for God and obedience to His call are to come first: before parents, before marriage and children. We are to submit these gifts for His greater purposes.

Consider the following Scriptures:

"He who loves father or mother more than Me is not worthy of Me; and he who loves son or daughter more than Me is not worthy of Me" (Matthew 10:37).

"If anyone comes to Me, and does not hate his own father and mother and wife and children and brothers and sisters, yes, and even his own life, he cannot be My disciple" (Luke 14:26).

The verse in Luke is particularly disturbing when we first read it. Does God really want us to "hate" our parents, our wife, our children, or our own life? No. Jesus was using a deliberate overstatement to make a point. We are to love God so much that our love for these dearest ones is like hate in comparison.

I struggled over these concepts in the past. I knew children of evangelists, pastors and missionaries who grew up embittered and angry at God seemingly because of their parents' ministries. Not all by any means. The majority of my friends who were raised in full-time Christian service went on to be strong Christians, many going into ministry themselves. But still there were the few, and the questions they raised remained in my heart, needling me from time to time.

A couple who were friends of our family went through the tragedy of their son turning away from God after they had spent years as missionaries in Africa. The anguished cry of that father echoed in my spirit: "I have won thousands of Africans to Jesus, and have lost my own son!"

That particular son later repented and is now himself a minister of the gospel. Still the question remains. Do the rigors and sacrifices of the ministry harm our children?

When our daughter, Karen, was a toddler I wrestled with this. The duties of our mission required me to be away for weeks at a time. We were living in a small apartment beside the first Youth With A Mission training school, in Lausanne, Switzerland, but I spent much of my time on the train or flying to and from the Geneva airport.

Besides preaching and sharing the news of our developing mission in churches around Western Europe, I was also making trips into Eastern Europe, preaching and on occasion, taking in Bibles. It was a risk, of course, and I worried. I knew God was telling me to do this, but what if I were arrested? Who would take care of Darlene and the kids? Was I being responsible? And what about these absences? Could I be a good father and husband and still obey God's call on my life?

Once, when Karen was thirteen months old, I came back and found she didn't know me. She wanted to stay in the arms of a friend, refusing to come to her own daddy. A knife blade turned in my chest, even though I reasoned she was much too young to know better.

A few years later, we noticed a clinging and fear in her and her little brother, David, each time I left on a trip. Once while I was away, a plane went overhead and David—two years old—pointed up and demanded they "let Daddy off!"

Another time I returned from a trip and had to make a quick jaunt back to the airport the same day to meet an arriving guest. Karen, then age four, asked her mom where I was.

Not thinking, Darlene said, "He's gone to the airport."

A moment later, Darlene turned and saw the tears spilling from Karen's eyes. Quickly, she added, "He went to pick up someone, not to leave."

Without missing a beat, Karen wiped away her tears. "I had something in my eye!" she said bravely.

It all just seemed too hard. I had been raised as a minister's son, and I knew that "ministry comes first." I never rebelled or turned away from God, even though my first memories were of living in a tent outside a little town in Arizona where my parents were pioneering a church. We had boxes for furniture, tin lids for plates, and my mom and dad were out every day making adobe bricks from mud, literally building their new church from dirt and sweat. But I did not grow up feeling deprived. In fact, my parents instilled in me a love for the gospel and the ministry. It was a privilege, not a sacrifice.

So how could I deal with this mounting feeling of deprivation in my children and in Darlene and me? More and more, I dreaded each trip and the pain of separation.

One year in early spring, I returned from yet another ministry trip. After a hurried breakfast, Dar bundled up Karen for preschool, then layered David with warm clothes and sent him outdoors to play. While I sat waiting for her to join me in the small sitting room, I watched David's chubby form through the window, busy with his toy trucks on the still-brown grass outside. He had changed so fast in the few weeks I had been away. I began to tick off the number of days we would enjoy before I had to leave again. There was so little time. Why did it have to be so difficult?

Dar came and snuggled beside me on the couch, tucking her feet under her.

"Loren, I've been doing a lot of praying about these separations we've been having," she began.

I sighed. "Yeah, honey. So have I." I knew she missed me and she especially worried when I went to Iron Curtain countries.

She hunched forward. "It doesn't have to be so bad, Loren! I think God has some keys for us, something to learn that will lighten the whole thing." She then began to tell me about a conversation she'd had with a co-worker while I was gone. Darlene confided in Joe Portale, one of the young leaders in our mission. She told Joe that she knew the Lord never allowed us to go through something hard that He had not gone through Himself while living on earth. That was part of His justice: He didn't ask us to give up rights that He Himself had not given up.

But Darlene questioned Joe. How could God understand the pain she felt in all our separations? Jesus was never married. How had He ever gone through this test? He wasn't even separated from the One who was closest to Him. Even while on earth Jesus said He and the Father were one.

She told me how Joe had reminded her that the Lord faced separation from His closest family member. When Jesus hung on the cross, He cried out, "My God, my God, why hast Thou forsaken Me?" For the first time in all of eternity, Jesus the Son felt the pain of separation from His Father as He took on all the sins of the world upon Himself. Our sins separated Him from His Father and He cried out with the pain of that awful loneliness.

Now Dar leaned excitedly toward me, her eyes filling with tears. "He knows how much we miss each other, Loren...He went through it, too!"

I reached around her narrow shoulders and held her tight. It was true, so true. We held each other and prayed in our little sitting room there in Switzerland. We each surrendered to God our right to be together, agreeing to go wherever He told us to go, as a family or separately. We prayed for Karen and David, telling God again, as we did when they were born, that they were His, not ours. We would be responsible for them but we would put them in His hands and trust Him with their lives.

A few days after our prayer in the sitting room, we were surprised with some remarkable gifts. A friend gave us a car for our use. Another man called from Holland and told us of a travel trailer which was available at an especially low price. Then some money came for us in the mail—exactly enough to buy the trailer. It seemed that these gifts were from the hand of the Lord. He had heard our relinquishing prayers and was giving us a way to be together more as I traveled in His work.

God also showed us other steps to take, for even though we had the trailer, there were times when I had to go alone. We led our children, young as they were, in the same step of relinquishing. Before my next trip, Darlene told the children I was to go and do something very important which God had told me to do—to preach and tell some people about Jesus. So there in our sitting room, with my bags packed and waiting by the door, Darlene and the children placed their hands on me and prayed for me, giving me to Jesus for this particular assignment. David piped in his two-year-old voice, "God, help Daddy preach good."

It made *all* the difference. There was a sense that the four of us were a team, and they were sending me out. When I picked up my bags to go, the fear of separation and the clinging of the children were gone.

Later, as my plane took off from the Geneva airport, I thought about that change. I realized then that their resentment over our separations had merely been a reflection of my own attitude! When I gave up my rights in this area, our four-year-old and two-year-old children relaxed and felt okay. A new security entered in: every member of our family was in God's hands, and He would take care of us.

I thought back over the individuals I had known who were embittered preacher's kids or missionary's kids. Were their reactions a reflection of their parents' feelings? Did they hear about the privilege of serving Jesus from their parents or did they hear about the sacrifices?

In the coming months, the Lord showed us more practical guidelines. I read 1 Kings 5:14, and I believed God showed me through this scripture a pattern for our planning. When the Lord asked Solomon to build His temple in Jerusalem, He gave him both a blueprint for the sanctuary and guidelines for the workmen. The men, who had to travel north to Lebanon to quarry stone for the temple, were sent for only one month at a time. Then they could come home to their families for two months before returning to their labors for God's temple.

I made it a rule to never be away from my family for more than thirty days at one time, and the total time away during a year should never exceed four months. Making this a priority has cost us thousands of dollars over the years, for at times I have flown back home from a continent halfway around the world, only to return very soon to the same continent. At other times it has meant taking my family with me, trusting God to provide four plane tickets instead of one.

A foolish expenditure of money? No, not when you realize the priority that God places on the family. God was always faithful to provide the money we needed to be together as a family, even though it meant us doing without things like owning a car or a house. Like everyone else in Youth With A Mission, Darlene and I have no salary. God has provided our needs, usually through the gifts of friends.

Sometimes His provision was dramatic, underscoring the importance He placed on not allowing our separations to be too long. Such was the time one winter when we were living in Hawaii, starting a YWAM school. I needed to be away for a total of two months for a circle of ministry in Europe, Thailand, Singapore and finally, Australia. I knew this would be breaking that rule we had set years before, of not being away from each other more than thirty consecutive days. Yet I didn't have enough money to take Darlene and the kids with me. In fact, I didn't have enough money for my entire trip: I only had enough to get me to Melbourne, Australia.

Darlene and I talked about it and prayed. What if she and the children could meet me in Australia, cutting our separation in half? We prayed again and were both convinced the Lord wanted us to plan on it. Somehow, we believed, God would make a way for her and the kids. And He would have to provide enough money for me to make it back to Hawaii from Melbourne.

Soon after that prayer, $100 came in the mail, but there was another YWAMer—Paul Hawkins—leaving on a different missionary trip. We believed God was impressing us to give Paul the $100. When the time came for me to leave, I set out for Europe with my partial ticket. A few days later, Dar reported another $100 came in. But she felt she was to give that away to one more individual in need.

Then a businessman telephoned Dar from Chicago. It was an acquaintance we hadn't heard from in a number of years. He asked Darlene if she and I were still living for God. How were we? Were we still in God's work?

She answered his questions, wondering why he had called after all these years.

The man closed the unexpected call by saying he just wanted to check on us because God had told him to do a certain thing. That was all.

A few days later, Darlene received a check from this same businessman. It was just the amount needed for three round-trip tickets to Australia!

Meanwhile, I was in Thailand. I spoke for a church there, and one of the men felt an unusual impression. They had never given money to westerners—this little church was more used to receiving missionary dollars than to giving them. This man stood and told the others in the Thai language that he felt they were to give me some money. It was enough to pay for my return to Hawaii from Melbourne, Australia. And since I couldn't legally enter Australia to meet my family without an onward air ticket, I was relieved and overjoyed.

The four of us rendezvoused in Australia, courtesy of our loving heavenly Father. That was a number of years ago. Now, our children are teenagers. Karen, nineteen, has obeyed God's call and gone with Youth With A Mission to Hong Kong and Taiwan for several months. David, our seventeen-year-old, recently stood with Karen at a gathering and surprised Darlene and me with a speech. He said, "Karen and I would like to thank you for being our parents. You've always been there for us. Never once did you push us aside while fulfilling the Great Commission. You're not just full-time missionaries; you're full-time parents!"

For family relationships, as with everything else in life, God's principle always works: We only win when we give up. As we grasp something, we lose it; when we surrender it to God, we gain it. If we hold our loved ones in a tight grip, we end up losing them. Putting any person first in our lives results in false expectations, disappointment and hurt, and finally alienation. Only God deserves to be first. It doesn't work any other way. If we surrender our families to God, we gain them. We reap new rewards of relationship—deeper relationship with God and, surprisingly, better relationships with family members.

You may be single and wondering what this has to do with you. Perhaps you have grown up, moved away from home and are longing for a family of your own. The same key—relinquishment—is just as true for you. You must give up your right to be married and embrace God's call on your life at this particular time. Then He can either release, in His right time, your mate for life, or He can give you greater privileges as a single to minister for Him.

I was single until I was twenty-seven, traveling from country to country as a missionary-evangelist. I longed for a wife and hated being alone. I remember standing on top of the Eiffel Tower, looking out over Paris. The view was stunning, and in my excitement I turned to remark on the beautiful panorama—but no one was there. I felt truly alone.

While I was still in Bible School, I had discovered the passage in 1 Corinthians 7 where Paul said it was a gift to be single. I sincerely hoped that God wasn't planning to give this gift to me! Time went by while I made some attempts on my own to figure out who was to be my life partner. I saw a wife as part of my necessary equipment as a minister, and there were always plenty of attractive candidates. But still, something was wrong. Then I came to understand that this scripture in 1 Corinthians was not to be skipped over and left for someone else. I reconsidered: Maybe God did want me to be single for the sake of His call on my life.

I responded by placing my right to be married on the altar. That was a phrase I learned from my parents—putting something on the "altar" was another way of saying, "I give up my rights." I told God, "Okay. I'm willing to never get married, if that is Your Will."

An amazing thing happened. There was a new freedom. No longer was I preoccupied with what I jokingly referred to as *The Search.* I was able to concentrate on what God wanted me to do next. A few months later, as I continued pursuing God's call on my life, my path crossed that of a vivacious blond in Redwood City, California. She had also just laid her desire to be married "on the altar." God brought us together.

Some people reject the idea of relinquishing to God their right to be married. Often times, they find themselves without inner peace because they cannot rest—they're always on the look out for "the right one," fretting over missed opportunities of the past, riddled with envy when a close friend gets married and "deserts" the single ranks. Those who never relinquish this right to God can find themselves in real trouble later on, when and if they *do* get married. When struggles and disagreements come, as they do for every married couple, they can be plagued by doubt. An inner voice can accuse: "You never *really trusted* God to show you your mate. What if you married the wrong person after all?"

How much better to give up the right to marriage to the Lord. In His right time, if He sees you can be more fulfilled and effective for Him with a life partner than without, He'll bring the very one that is right for you and for His Kingdom. In any case, as a Christian you will want to have the confidence of knowing that your marriage is firmly fixed in the center of His will. And let me assure you: He will choose a better wife or husband for you than you can. He sure can pick them! I am a witness to that!

CHAPTER FOUR

Almighty God— Or the Almighty Dollar?

Money is one of God's most useful good gifts. Are you surprised?

But isn't money the root of all evil? No, read the scriptures again. In 1 Timothy 6:10 Paul says "The *love* of money is the root of all evils…."

God never said money was evil. He gave us the right to own material things, to have personal possessions. One of the Ten Commandments is, "Thou shalt not steal." This shows the importance God put on the right of ownership.

Certain cults deny people this right. They demand newcomers sign over all their wealth and property "to God." The inference is that owning things is wrong and displeasing to God, and that the only way to please Him is to own nothing.

In every lie of Satan there is a grain of truth. God does love a cheerful giver, and throughout history there have been Christian groups who have forsaken all to follow Jesus. But let no human being demand that you give up all earthly possessions before you can "follow God."

On the other hand, the Lord *may* lead you to give everything you have. But even if you give all time and again, don't let go of the joy of giving.

In 1971, when Darlene and I were leading that first missionary training school in Lausanne, Switzerland, we believed God was telling us to buy the hotel which we were renting for the school. It was the first property our fledgling organization tried to buy and it was quite a stretching experience for our faith. We needed thousands of dollars.

God led us and our group of staff and students through many steps of obedience as we prayed and trusted Him for the money. One step which God required of Darlene and me was to give everything we owned. My parents had helped us buy a house in California, several years before. We kept it rented out to cover the payments each month—it was our only nest egg. Darlene and I sold this house, paid off the indebtedness and gave the balance, along with all the money we had in the bank at the time, towards the purchase of the hotel in Switzerland.

We bought the hotel in June of 1971, as God brought in contributions from other friends throughout the world to add to what our little group had scraped together. But the story didn't end there. For the next fifteen years, Darlene, the children and I continued to live wherever we were working with our mission—sometimes in one room, other times in two or three rooms at a training center. We didn't think of it as a sacrifice to not own a house.

Then in early 1986, God spoke to us about buying our own home. It seemed ridiculous—we didn't have any money or ability to buy one, but in various ways God told us that we would own our own home soon. One of the scriptures that spoke directly to me was in Proverbs 13, where it says a good man leaves an inheritance for his children's children.

Unknown to us, a young YWAMer named Matthew Nocas from the training center in Lindale, Texas, went to his leaders, Leland and Fran Paris, with an idea—he wanted to give and get the thousands of others in our organization to give to buy us a house. The idea was to honor us and show us a practical demonstration of the love of more than 6,500 full-time YWAM workers around the world. They set up a trust and for many months secretly collected love gifts from our friends.

What happened next was a most humbling, happy time for me and my family. We were invited for a special evening in a lovely hotel ballroom in Kona, Hawaii. More than seven hundred gathered for what they called *Operation Honor.* Many of our friends talked about their love for us, some speaking in their native tongues of Tongan, Swahili, Arabic, Portuguese, Indonesian and others.

Then, when our hearts were bursting with the emotion of it all, they brought out the architectural drawings and building plans for a beautiful house, for which they had purchased property in Kona! We were overwhelmed—stunned, wanting to cry and laugh at the same time. Then they flung open the double-door at one side of the ballroom and there was a new Nissan sedan—the first car of our own in more than twenty years. I sat there shaking my head in disbelief while Darlene whooped like a game show contestant.

The immediate impact of the evening was the almost embarrassing display of love and gratitude from the ones we loved and appreciated so much. Later it sank in that God was also repaying our obedience to Him fifteen years earlier when we sold our nest egg to buy our first mission property. And He was giving us something to leave behind for our children.

You see, even if you give everything you have, God will return it to you so that you will always have the joy of giving. He promises this explicitly in Mark 10:29, 30. Ownership is a right and a responsibility which He has given you.

Jesus talked about money more than any other topic. In fact, one out of six of His statements recorded in the Gospels pertained to financial matters. Jesus talked about money more than He talked about salvation, Heaven, the Church or the Kingdom of God. Why did Jesus give such attention to money? I believe it is because He knew how close our wallets are to our hearts! Martin Luther said that the last thing to get converted is most often a person's pocketbook.

One-third of Jesus' parables were about money or possessions. The Parable of the Talents in Matthew 25 was one. Often we hear this parable used to talk about other talents—*skills*, like piano playing or public speaking. But we must remember it was money that Jesus was talking about in this passage. We could call it the Parable of the Dollars.

A talent weighed approximately seventy-five pounds. Assuming that these were gold talents, we can figure that when Jesus said one servant was given five talents, He was talking about over $2 million dollars in today's terms! The point of the parable was that we are expected to wisely use our resources, investing money for the Kingdom of God.

Most Christians have no problem understanding their God-given right to ownership. What is out of balance is our willingness to obey God in giving. Instead of worshipping Almighty God, we worship the Almighty Dollar.

The Lord has given us people to love and things to use, but too often we love things and use people.

Perhaps you know someone with an expensive sports car. He spends hours maintaining and polishing it. He parks carefully, at a diagonal across two parking spots, lest someone open a car door next to his prized vehicle and scratch the finish. Only a certain garage can handle his vehicle; only a special service can be trusted to wash it. Have you ever thought that the car seemed to be driving him rather than vice versa?

It's easy to smile over others' excesses, but what about our own? A friend of mine said that you could read anyone's checkbook and see what they were living for. Jesus stood at the treasury and watched the people giving. What does He see in your checkbook? What is the pattern of your giving to Him and His work?

Some may think all of this doesn't apply to them. Didn't Jesus say it was harder for the rich to enter Heaven? You may say, "I'm always broke. I'm just a student." Or, "I'm out of a job—God can't be telling me to give."

Don't think that because you are poor you cannot be serving money rather than God. I have seen just as much bondage to ownership in Third World countries where the average per capita income is below poverty level. There, the bondage may be to a bicycle rather than a Porsche, or to a transistor radio instead of a compact disc player. For the poor, the lust to own and the fear to release are just as strong, if not stronger. The poor lust so much after things that they are kept in financial bondage—rather than saving money so that it can be multiplied, they often fall into debt with a "get-it-now" mentality.

The rich, on the other hand, are freer from money. Their temptation is more often for the power and control that their money can buy them. Have you ever seen someone who wants to make a large gift to the church *provided they start doing things their way?*

All God wants is for us to relax our grip on what we own, to open our hand and allow Him to use what He has placed in it. He says we can't be a servant to money and a servant to Him at the same time. He gives us the right to own things and then asks us to give back to Him freely what He has blessed us with. Since God truly owns everything anyway—including whatever He has allowed us to have—we have the choice to either be a good steward or to be a thief and steal from Him. The late R.G. LeTourneau, a man made wealthy by his invention of various earth-moving equipment, put it this way: "It's not how much of *my* money that I give to God that counts. It's how much of *His* money I keep for myself."

Only as we give up the right to spend our money as we want will we see God as our provider. When we say to God, "Tell me what you want. All I have is yours. How do you want me to use it for you?"—only then will we have the excitement of seeing Him do the miraculous to meet our needs. Only then will we understand the security of being a child of God that transcends any layoff, any recession, any market slump—even famine!

There was a widow once, a single mother raising her son alone. They were broke, and for some time they had not had enough to eat. Both suffered from malnutrition. The little boy had the matchstick legs and arms and the bloated stomach of starvation, and the mother could barely drag herself around to take care of his needs. There was just enough food left to make one tiny meal. She planned to prepare that—a small loaf of bread—and then she would lie down with her little boy and wait for death.

She was foraging for some sticks, building a fire to cook the loaf when she was approached by a stranger. He was a man of God, named Elijah. He wanted something to eat. She must have stood there, swaying a little in her hunger, wondering how this man could ask her for what little she had. Couldn't he see her cloudy eyes, her drawn face? And what about her son, lying at home on his pallet, not even strong enough to wave away the flies? For weeks, in her quiet, mounting panic, she had listened to his pitiful cries.

Yet at the moment when the man of God challenged her to give, something must have rallied within her. Some spark that said, "Yes, give it away! What do you have to lose?"

She did sacrifice and you probably know the rest of the story. She gave that last handful of flour and few drops of oil, and Elijah ate her loaf of bread. Then he left her and the boy with an abundant provision of food for the future. But the key was this: She had to give up the right to her possessions before God was able to meet her own need.

There are enormous needs in the world today. God is not deaf to the cries of 750 million who go to sleep every night with their stomachs gnawed with hunger. He knows the name of every one of the 20 million children who will curl up to sleep on the pavements of South American cities tonight. He wept over the frail bodies of the 40,000 children who died yesterday from hunger. He sees the twenty-one who will die of hunger in the time it takes you to read this sentence. He knows the desperate who are homeless on the streets of America—the families who are huddled to sleep in cars, or under the overpasses of our freeways. He watches the 900 million around the world who will sleep in shanties of cardboard or scrap tin tonight and the 100 million who will lie down without any roof at all over their heads. He knows those who are without any form of sanitation, who forage in the world's garbage dumps, those who die for the lack of cheap, simple medicines, those who have no school where they can send their children and no future to look forward to.

As gut-wrenching as these needs are, they are only part of the story. How much Christ must weep over the 100,000 who die every day without having heard His name! He knows by name every individual among the 2.5 billion worldwide waiting to hear the gospel. Why doesn't He do something to finance the job of world evangelization? If God could create manna and rain down food for several million of His people in the wilderness, can't He produce enough money for His people to meet the physical and spiritual needs of the world today?

I believe He already has. God has placed enough resources in the hands of Christians to fully evangelize the billions in the world who have never heard the name of Jesus Christ. He has given us enough to preach the gospel and to meet physical needs as well. The funds are already there—like a handful of meal and a drop or two of oil in a bottle, waiting to be multiplied and given out to feed a hungry world. Let me give some examples:

- Dr. David Barrett, researcher and editor of *The World Christian Encyclopedia,* reports there are 1.68 billion people who name the name of Christ. Christians have annual incomes totaling approximately U.S. $8.2 trillion and own two-thirds of the earth's resources.

- It would take each person who calls himself Christian only $1 to place a Bible in every home on earth. (Based on earth's population of 5 billion, an average of five people to a home, and the cost of less than $1 per copy of the Bible.)

- There are 2,000 unreached ethno-linguistic groups in the world. If only 40 million Christians gave $1 a year, we could support two missionaries for each of these groups.

- For the cost of caring for a pet dog or a cat for a year, a child in the Third World could be given a Christian education.

- There are 16 million refugees in the world, according to most sources. To feed every one of those refugees, it would only cost the 1.6 billion who call themselves Christians one penny a day.

You can see that when I say God has already given us the money to evangelize the world, it is literally true—and at no great sacrifice, either! God wants to meet every person's need—spiritual and physical. He wants to involve us in meeting that need. He could do it without us. He could have fed Elijah without the widow's handful of meal and cruse of oil. And he did feed Elijah supernaturally at one point by sending ravens with food. But God wanted to bless the woman and share with her the excitement of seeing a miracle performed on her behalf.

You may have a desire in your heart to give, but are continually frustrated when you hear of financial needs. Every day may bring missionary newsletters to your door, each presenting legitimate needs. How can you know to whom to give and how much? I believe the only key to this frustration is to listen to the voice of the Lord in your giving—give out of obedience to Him, not out of your emotion. A story from some close friends of mine will show what I mean.

A number of years ago, a group of young people was leaving southern California on a YWAM outreach to

Hawaii. My friends, Jim and Joy Dawson, are among the most spiritually-attuned people I know. They had gone to the Los Angeles Airport to see the youth off because their son and daughter were part of the team. When they walked in, they found two–Steve and Verna—sitting forlornly in the terminal. This pair was on the list of those who were to leave, but Joy found out they didn't have enough money to buy their tickets—they were each $100 short.

Both Steve and Verna felt God was telling them to go on this mission venture and had come with their bags packed as an act of faith and obedience.

Joy prayed with her husband—though they had already given several hundred dollars to others leaving on this team, they were willing to give to these two if God directed them to do so. As the Dawsons bowed their heads in the terminal, they asked the Lord if they were to give more.

The Lord impressed both of them, however, that they were not to give. The words that Joy received in her mind were, *You've done your part. I want to provide for these two through someone else.*

There was nothing to do but stand back and let the drama unfold. They watched the clock. The flight was due to leave at 6:00 P.M. and there were only minutes left.

Then a voice came over the P.A. system.

"Western Airlines, flight #771 leaving for Honolulu, now boarding at Gate 63."

The group, minus Steve and Verna, filed down the jet bridge. Six o'clock came and passed. Yet Jim and Joy watched through the airport's smoked-glass windows as the big plane sat unmoving. Why weren't they leaving? The uniformed airline agent still stood behind the desk at the gate, the empty jet bridge yawning at his back. No voice came over the P.A. to explain the delay.

Jim looked at his watch. It was now 6:15.

Just then, a young YWAMer, Clay Golliher, came rushing into the terminal. He was panting, his face damp and red. "Has the plane left for Hawaii?" he gasped. "God told me to give some money to the team leaving for Hawaii." He nodded to Steve and Vernal "Do you need some money?"

"Yes," Steve said. "We each need $100."

Clay reached into his pocket and pulled out a white envelope. "Then I guess this is for you two!"

Steve and Verna thanked him, grabbed the money and ran to the airlines personnel. At first they refused them. It was too late, they were told. Everyone else was on the plane and besides, it was already past the departure time!

Jim Dawson got into the act, persuading the officials to bend a little and let the two young people join their friends on the plane.

"They're going on a missionary trip," Jim offered.

Finally the airlines people gave in. Tickets were hastily written out and Steve and Verna ran down the jet bridge, carrying their suitcases on board with them.

Clay, Jim and Joy watched as the big plane slowly pulled away. Then they heard Clay's side of the story.

Clay had been in another part of L.A. that afternoon, at the Philippine Consulate, getting a visa for his own missionary trip. As he crossed the marble lobby to leave, God's voice came clearly into his mind, *You don't need that extra spending money you have for your trip.*

The Lord impressed him that he was to give it to the team leaving for Hawaii that evening. He looked at a clock on the wall of the office building—2:30!—and he knew the group was leaving at 6:00. He rushed out of the building and began looking for a bus. He hopped aboard and slowly made his way across L.A. in fits and starts. Finally, he was deposited on Foothill Boulevard in Sunland, one block away from the YWAM Center.

Clay ran to the building, but his heart sank at the sight of the empty parking lot. There was one car, however. The doors to the center were all locked, but he went around banging on the side doors, the front and back doors. A boy came to the door dripping wet. He had been in the shower. He told Clay the Hawaii team had left an hour before. At Clay's urging, the boy dressed and the two got into the car and headed to the airport, fighting the L.A rush hour traffic on the freeways. At last, they arrived at the curb in front of the Western terminal—well after the flight's departure time.

Clay stopped his story and began to laugh with Jim and Joy. There were so many improbable incidents in his account: a bus just at the right time in a city known for its lack of buses; one lone guy left behind, taking a shower, who happened to have a car; the unexplained delay of the plane until after Clay got there. How much they would have missed, they all agreed, if Jim and Joy had reacted out of their emotions and given the money to the two.

So many times we miss the excitement of giving because we don't listen to the Lord and obey Him.

When our motivation in giving is to obey and please our heavenly Father, then we will be free from other temptations that often come with financial appeals. On the one hand, we can avoid the greed that is often appealed to. ("Give to God and He will give you more!") We can also avoid the trap of manipulation (giving in order to control others) and the trap of a prideful motive (giving in order to have our name engraved on a plaque on the front of the building). Nor should we fall prey to appeals that work on our guilt: ("If you don't give now, this ministry will cease and millions will go to Hell!")

Instead, we can give out of a pure heart, obeying the promptings of the Holy Spirit. Then we will see God as our provider as well.

In Youth With A Mission we have seen many financial miracles for those who have given all. We have a slogan, **You do the possible, then God will do the impossible.** Dean and Michelle Sherman were YWAMers in Hilo, Hawaii, trusting God for the money to meet the needs of their young family. They were broke and had just run out of formula for their baby. Michelle prayed, then she and Dean walked home to their apartment from the training center.

On the way, Michelle stopped and stared at a bush beside a busy road. She could scarcely believe her eyes! For there on the plant were crisp one- and five-dollar bills, each bill lying neatly across a different branch! Dean and Michelle picked them all off and counted—it was $35, enough to buy formula and a baby carrier like Michelle had been wanting. You might say they literally found money growing on a tree! God had used an extraordinary method to meet their need.

More often, though, God uses other people to meet our needs. He does this to encourage interdependence in the body of Christ.

How many have money they could give, but are waiting to get a little more secure, to invest a little more first, to have a few more basic "necessities" of their own met? How often does God speak to us to give and we shrug it off, rationalizing the impression away?

Years ago I was in New Zealand, speaking at a Youth For Christ retreat that drew together young people from many backgrounds. Along with teenagers from local churches, there were some new Christians who were making decisions to leave behind alcohol or drug addictions and serve Christ, and even some who had never accepted Jesus as Lord.

It was after one of these meetings that I took a walk before going to bed. I left behind the scattered buildings of the camp and walked toward the country road, enjoying the moonlit outline of trees and nearby sheep paddocks. An impression came into my mind and I stopped on the dirt path. I recognized the still small voice of God: *Loren, what do you have in your pocket?*

I reached in and drew out some bills and change.

Looking up at the sky, I held it out. "I have some money, Lord."

So many exciting things had been happening at this conference. I was ready to do anything God told me.

Throw your money down on the ground! the inner voice said.

Quickly, I tossed it down and walked on, wondering what on earth God would do with my money. I imagined a scenario of a person with some urgent need, praying and finding my money.

Before I got very far, God surprised me and spoke again in my mind. *Go back and pick it up, Loren.* I tried to ignore it, supposing it was just my thoughts, but the impression grew in intensity. Finally, I retraced my steps back along the path, knelt down, felt around for all the scattered coins and bills and shoved them into my pocket.

I straightened up and disappointedly turned back towards the camp. As I came into the lighted area, a figure was walking toward me. I could make out the face and stringy dark hair of a teenager who was approaching me. I had been counseling with him earlier that day and knew he was a drug addict. Again the Voice came in my mind. *Give all the money in your pocket to him.*

I argued with God just long enough for the teenager to pass me and disappear into the darkness. As I kept walking, I pointed out to the Lord that this fellow couldn't be trusted. He might use the money for drugs. Anyway, he was gone. Probably by now he was already in his room, and I didn't know where that was.

But God wouldn't let me forget His orders. "All right, Lord," I sighed. "If this is really you, have that same guy be there when I walk back around this building."

I circled the cinderblock structure and nearly bumped into the same young guy coming around the corner. Finally, I obeyed God and handed him all my money. In the light of an outdoor lantern, I watched as he began to cry in amazement.

Then he spoke quietly, "I just told God I would go to that Christian drug rehabilitation place if He would give me the money! I had some. But with this," he shook his head in wonder, fingering the bills and coins, "there's exactly enough to get there!" Smiling, he pumped my hand and left.

I stood there, rooted to the ground in shame. I had been willing to throw money onto the road and walk away, but I had clutched it tightly when I didn't agree with God's direction to invest it in this young man.

What is in your pocket right now? Are you willing to let God tell you what to do with it? Are you willing to let Him rule you and your wallet, or do you hold back as I did that night in New Zealand?

Those who are willing to give freely as the Lord leads will be allowed the privilege of seeing God multiply their resources to reach the world.

CHAPTER FIVE

I Am What I Am

Bill McChesney was an American missionary, killed at age twenty-eight in the Congo uprising of 1964. Before he went to the Congo, he wrote the following poem:

My Choice

I want my breakfast served at "Eight,"
With ham and eggs upon the plate;
A well-broiled steak I'll eat at "One,"
And dine again when day is done.

I want an ultra modern home,
And in each room a telephone;
Soft carpets, too, upon the floors,
And pretty drapes to grace the doors.

A cozy place of lovely things,
Like easy chairs with innersprings,
And then I'll get a small TV—
Of course, "I'm careful what I see."

I want my wardrobe, too, to be
Of neatest, finest quality,
With latest style in suit and vest.
Why shouldn't Christians have the best?

But then the Master I can hear,
In no uncertain voice, so clear,
"I bid you come and follow me,
The Lowly Man of Galilee."

"Birds of the air have made their nest,
And foxes in their holes find rest;
But I can offer you no bed;
No place have I to lay my head."

In shame I hung my head and cried,
How could I spurn the Crucified ?
Could I forget the way He went,
The sleepless nights in prayer He spent?

For forty days without a bite,
Alone He fasted day and night;
Despised, rejected—on He went,
And did not stop till veil He rent.

A Man of sorrows and of grief,
No earthly friend to bring relief—
"Smitten of God," the prophet said—
Mocked, beaten, bruised, His blood ran red.

If He be God and died for me,
No sacrifice too great can be
For me, a mortal man, to make;
I'll do it all for Jesus' sake.

Yes, I will tread the path He trod,
No other way will please my God;
So, henceforth, this my choice shall be,
My choice for all eternity.

You were born to your parents, raised in a neighborhood, brought up to believe certain beliefs and to salute one flag. You heard stories of your past and your country. Your mom fixed food in a particular way, and those dishes probably remain among your favorite foods to this day. Whether you are an American, a Filipino or a Swiss, whether you grew up in New York or New Delhi, these things are part of what makes you *you*.

When you need something to wear you go out and buy what you like. That will likely be influenced by the way others you admire dress themselves. If you live in the West, it could be an outfit like you've seen everyone else wearing on television; if you live in a Malaysian village, it could be a certain way to tie a hand-dyed sarong. Whatever it is, you are happier and feel you are at your best dressed a certain way, eating a certain food, living in a certain kind of house and raising your children to do the things that are important to you.

Even where you go to church is special, geared to your background, your choices, your likes and dislikes and your experiences. You may like a plain building for worship with happy, informal singing and preaching that makes you want to cry. Or you might like stained-glass windows and a soaring pipe organ. Your minister may emphasize

God's control over everything and God's sovereignty is an idea that comforts you. Or you may prefer to hear about the free will of man and your own responsibility to get right with God.

These are all parts of your culture, your heritage, your denomination, your family and your upbringing.

You have the right to your American culture (or Australian or Brazilian or Russian). You have the right to enjoy your culture and love your country. You have the right to belong to a certain church and to other groups that express what you believe is important. You have a right to live, talk, eat and dress in a way that is comfortable to you and to those around you.

But if everyone exercises these rights *to the exclusion of God's plans for us and for our lives,* a tragedy of cataclysmic proportions will certainly take place. Hundreds of millions of people will live out their lives in emptiness and despair. They will die and face certain judgment for their sins, eternally separated from God in Hell. All we have to do to seal the fate of these billions is to stay where we are, in surroundings comfortable to us, shutting our ears to God's cry, "Whom shall I send and who will go for Me?"

A young man once came up to General William Booth, the founder of the Salvation Army.

"Sir," the young man began, "I don't know what to do with my life. I've never had a call."

General Booth squared his broad shoulders and fixed his eye on the young man. "What? You've never *had* a call?" boomed the bearded evangelist. "You mean you've never *heard* the call!"

The Bible says, in Mark 16:15 KJV, "Go ye into all the world, and preach the gospel to every creature." In John 15:16 KJV, the Lord says, "I have chosen you, and ordained you, that ye should go and bring forth fruit…"

I believe each of us is either a missionary or a mission field. We are either part of God's answer or part of His problem. We're either an asset or a liability to the Kingdom of God.

You might be asking yourself, "How can I be a missionary?" First, get a clear idea of what a missionary is. It is not just someone wearing a pith helmet, standing under a tree preaching to natives. The word *missionary* means "one who is sent." Jesus has said to every one of us, "As the Father has sent me, even so I send you" (John 20:21). That means you are a missionary regardless of your geography.

If you are living in the will of God, you are a missionary on the job wherever you work. If you're not there to be a missionary, you are like those Jesus described as putting their light under a bushel, which is a symbol of material abundance. You have been sent to your neighborhood as a missionary. If you are not representing Jesus Christ to those living on your block, you're like the one who put his candle under a bed, which symbolizes ease and comfort.

If you are still in school, God wants you to be His missionary right there in your classroom and on your campus. John 1:6 says, "There was a man sent from God, whose name was John." Take this verse, and repeat it aloud to yourself right now, inserting your name: *(There was a man/woman sent from God whose name was* __________ .)

Your next step is to ask God if you are serving as a missionary in the place where He wants you. Don't just assume that you are to stay where you are.

A few years ago, I became friends with a young Christian musician named Keith Green. I was impressed by this intense young man. He seemed like a coiled spring, full of energy and ready to hurl himself into any venture he believed in. He was also humble and full of questions for me, as one who had ministered longer. He was so hungry to know more of God.

In 1982, he and his wife, Melody, went on a trip to the mission field and came home fired up with zeal for reaching the billions of lost people who are without Jesus.

After their return, our two families got together at a friend's beach cottage on the California coast. It was a cool, overcast morning and sea gulls swooped outside the large windows overlooking the beach. Outside, our teenagers, Karen and David, played with Keith and Melody's kids—little three-year-old Josiah and Bethany, age two. We adults sat inside on the floor, talking for hours about missions. Keith's intense desire was to do whatever he could to mobilize the thousands of young people who were coming to his concerts.

Then we began to pray earnestly. Keith was lying face down on the carpet, crying out for lost souls. We asked God for 100,000 young people to go out as missionaries from America—especially those who were eighteen and nineteen years of age. We committed ourselves to God and to one another, to do whatever we could to further this goal. We planned to launch a special missions concert tour together in the fall.

Two weeks after the time of our prayer beside the beach, Keith was dead, along with little Josiah, Bethany and nine others, in the crash of his small plane in Texas. I was in Japan on an evangelism outreach when I heard of his death, and I immediately remembered our prayer for young missionaries. As I met with several of our workers to pray, the scripture about a grain of wheat falling into the ground in order to die and spring forth in a harvest one hundred times greater than itself came into our minds.

That fall we went ahead with the missions concerts even though Keith had gone to be with Jesus. Many thousands of young people watched a video of one of his last concerts and heard his final appeal to give all and go. During that videotaped message, Keith said,

> *"It's not God's fault that the world isn't being won. It's not His will that any should perish. There's a little command in the Bible that says, 'Go ye into all the world and preach the gospel to every creature.'*
>
> *"We like to think that was for the disciples, for the missionaries, for old ladies that can't find husbands that need to bury their troubles on the mission field, or for humanitarians, for real Christians that are so spiritual they can't stay in society so they go overseas....*
>
> *"The world isn't being won because we're not doing it. It's our fault. Nowhere on earth is the gospel as plentiful as it is here in the United States. You don't need a call—you've already had one. If you stay [in America] you better be able to say to God, 'You called me to stay home.' If you don't have a definite call to stay here, you are called."*

Strong words. But are they true?

There are only 250,000 Protestant and Catholic missionaries trying to reach those who have not yet heard the gospel. And yet there are 1.2 million Avon representatives worldwide and over 750,000 Amway distributors. We have visited remote villages as the *very first ones* to carry in the gospel, and yet we have found Coca Cola and Singer sewing machines were there ahead of us.

Is it God's will that so many haven't heard His Word yet? Is this the way He has planned it? Did He call 94 percent of the full-time ministers to reach 9 percent of the world's population (those in the English-speaking world)? Or did He direct that 92 percent of all Christian finances for evangelism be spent to evangelize in the United States where only 8 percent of the world's population lives, where many have already heard the gospel many times over?

Even in North America, there are great, gaping holes of spiritual darkness. Most Christian effort and finances are spent in the areas of greatest Christian population, leaving places like American inner cities with less gospel witness than many mission fields.

You can see that something is very much out of balance, and I agree with my friend, Keith. It's not God's plan for things to remain this way. We have to be willing to answer God's call and say, "Here am I, Lord, send me… anywhere!" We have to be willing to give up the right to stay at home.

Abram gave up the right to stay in his own country. When God's call came to him, he had a good job in his father's business. God told him to pack up; he was going to a new country.

"Where, Lord?" he asked. And God replied, "I'll tell you on the way."

What extraordinary faith this required of him. He had to say goodbye to his friends and he couldn't even tell them where he was going! By the way, according to Jewish tradition, the profession of Abram's father was making idols. Like any son of that time, Abram must have worked in his father's trade. So, Abram could have said no to God and kept on making idols.

Are you saying "No" or, "Maybe later" to God's call? Search your heart to be sure that you are not in the idol making business, too!

You see, it's so easy to make idols of things like nice clothes, homes, good looks, comfort, ease and pleasure. If we're not careful, these good gifts of God become the object of our pursuit—little gods!

Paul Rader was a big, strapping football player who lived in the early part of this century. He became an imposing figure on Wall Street, where he headed City Service Oil Company. Then he got saved and obeyed God's call to preach, finding a post as an assistant pastor in Pittsburgh. Paul Rader would have been appalled if someone had told him there were still false gods in his life.

One week, a visiting speaker came to his church. Paul took one look at the man, a missionary, and shook his head in disgust. First of all, the man was wearing a flimsy-looking suit of wrinkled brown silk. When he began to talk it was in a soft, delicate voice. He seemed a little frail. *Not like a real man at all,* thought Rader. As he spoke about his work in China, he often dabbed at the corners of his mouth with a handkerchief.

Paul approached the man after the meeting and challenged him. "Sir, why are you so sissified? You call yourself a man of God, but look at the way you're dressed and the way you talk. I don't think you're much of a missionary!"

The man patiently explained. "I'm sorry about this suit, but I have ministered in China for twenty-five years. When it was time to leave, all my western clothes had been worn out for years. The believers in my village pooled their resources to buy the silk to make me this suit, shirt and tie. They didn't have a machine so they stitched it by hand."

He dabbed at his mouth again and Rader's disgust must have shown on his face, for the missionary continued. "As for my voice...I did a lot of street preaching and was often beaten up. One time a gang took turns beating me and a man jumped on my throat. My larynx is permanently damaged and I no longer have control of my salivary glands."

Embarrassed now, Rader murmured an apology and hastened to find a place alone. He went down to the church basement, found a pile of coal and stretched out on it, face down. He cried out to God, begging forgiveness for his attitude. He told the Lord he wanted to serve Him like this man.

From that day on, Paul Rader was a man with a missionary heart. As a pastor and leader in the Christian Missionary Alliance, he influenced many thousands of young men and women to give themselves for missions.

Along with a willingness to go, Jesus wants you to be ready to be molded and used in any way He needs your service. Jesus doesn't promise the comforts of home, or the latest of fashion. His soldiers don't always have a soft bed, and sometimes they have no bed at all. In the mission I am part of, we have thousands of young people who are sleeping in hammocks or air mattresses, trekking into dense jungles or mountainous regions for days or weeks to find hidden tribes, all for the purpose of introducing Jesus.

One such young person is Braulia Riberio. A bright, pert twenty-five-year-old like Braulia doesn't appear to be a courageous soldier, yet that's what she is.

Braulia was raised in a middle-class Brazilian home, but since 1983, she has been working as a YWAM missionary among the Indian tribes on the Amazon. When Braulia and her team members leave their base camp and go up river, it often takes many weeks of river navigation by boat, then small canoes, followed by hikes into the jungles to get to a tribe that no outsider has visited before.

There they stay, without outside contact, while they work on the laborious task of learning to communicate with the Indians.

For years, Braulia has existed on $50 a month missionary support. This is typical for our Brazilian YWAMers, and yet they manage to carry on in aggressive evangelism. While in the jungle away from their base camp, they eat whatever they can hunt or fish or whatever the Indians give them. This is often roasted monkey, rat or snake meat. They sleep in the Indians' huts with them, knowing no privacy or modern comforts. The realities of the Amazon include leeches; humid, sticky days and nights; mosquitos; poisonous snakes and insects.

Life-threatening danger is always a possibility in the Amazon, especially when you're approaching an Indian group for the first time. It isn't unusual for outsiders to be murdered by the fearful natives.

Braulia and her team tried not to think about that when they went in to make the first visit to the Zuiruaha tribe. They learned of this group's existence through other tribes, and went to the area where they were told the Zuiruaha could be found.

Deep in the jungle, they were suddenly surrounded by fierce-looking men. The Indians' naked bodies were painted red with some sort of dye, and they were carrying bows and arrows, which the YWAMers guessed to be poison-tipped. Braulia tried to gesture to them, to assure them they just wanted to be their friends. But the Indians just stared at them, circling warily.

Then they grabbed the workers, ripped off their clothes and began smearing them with the same red dye. What were they going to do? Would they be killed? Braulia and the others were entirely at their mercy. One of the girls started to cry.

After half an hour, the Indians decided to give their clothes back. Then they understood that the Zuiruaha were just trying to welcome them and make them a part of their tribe. They were brought into the village and the mission of Jesus Christ to the Zuiruaha of the Amazon was underway.

In the Amazon, when an emergency happens, they are often isolated and have to trust in their own wits and God's power to help them.

On a subsequent visit to the Zuiruaha, Braulia and a girl named Hulda were dropped off by a river boat guide to trek in for twenty-four hours to find the village again. Their guide agreed to return with messages and supplies in thirty-five days.

But after one week, Braulia's friend, Hulda, was stricken with a severe attack of malaria. Their little supply of medicine was soon exhausted. They had no radio to call for medical help—they'd never had the funds to buy one. After the girl got so weak that she couldn't get off her hammock for ten days, it became apparent to Braulia that Hulda would die soon without help.

Braulia and some of the Indians hiked a day and a night to get back to the place on the river where their guide had left them. Braulia stood anxiously scanning the broad waters, hoping to see a boat. There was none. It was another two weeks before their river guide was due to return, but Braulia hoped against hope that someone would pass by.

A day went by and the Indians were impatient to return. Braulia stood on the river bank in desperation, knowing her friend would die and not knowing what to do to help her. Then God spoke to her. "Go back to the village. I'll take care of Hulda."

Braulia hung up a hand-lettered sign beside the river, asking for help and leaving trail directions on how to find them. Then she returned to the village.

Somehow, Hulda survived another two and a half weeks. Their guide returned at the appointed time, found Braulia's sign and hiked into the village, carrying Hulda out in his arms. Still, it took them another seventeen days navigating the rivers before they reached a small town with a doctor! Hulda had been sick for over forty days, but she recovered.

This was just one adventure. Braulia recently married, and now she and her husband are continuing the ministry to the Zuiruaha. Their goal is to translate the Bible into the Zuiruaha language.

The workers on the Amazon are just a few of the thousands of young soldiers working around the world in incredible situations to get the gospel out. We also have teams living on the edge of a huge garbage dump in Manila, Philippines, working among the 10,000 squatters who live there. Others have been working in Beirut, Lebanon, on the border of Thailand in refugee camps and in many, many other places of danger and hardship. Yet if you were to meet these young people, you would not see martyrs or mystics. They are young people caught up with the thrill and privilege of what they're doing. They don't focus on the tropical heat nor the size of the insects, but on the excitement of seeing God use them to make a radical difference among people! Like Jesus, they endure suffering for the greater prize that is set before them.

In the early part of this century, an ad appeared in a London newspaper: *Men wanted for hazardous journey; small wages, bitter cold, long months of complete darkness, constant danger. Safe return doubtful. Honor and recognition in case of success.*

The ad was signed by Sir Ernest Shackleton, Antarctic explorer. And thousands responded to the call.

I believe there are hundreds of thousands of young people who are just waiting for a really challenging, dangerous job that requires them to give up everything. You may be one. The reward? Being a part of the climaxing event of all history—taking the gospel to every person on earth.

Giving up the right to being comfortable at home is just one area of dedication to the Lord. You may be called upon to work with people who are not like you, who think differently than you do. In many ways that's even harder.

There is nothing wrong with going to the church where you feel most comfortable, where everyone believes as you do. But what happens when you move out in ministry and God calls you to work with someone else? Perhaps you have wide differences of opinion with them politically or, worse yet, doctrinally! What then? Aren't we all to strive to keep the faith pure? How can we work with people who believe differently than we do? Aren't we supposed to guard against heresy and apostasy?

I have come to the conviction that the *spirit* behind an issue is more crucial than *differences in understanding.* The spirit of heresy is *adding to* what is truth. The spirit of apostasy is *taking from* truth.

How many of us understand *all* truth? Is there any believer in the Lord Jesus Christ who would say, "Yes, I know it all!" Every Christian believes he is in the middle of the road doctrinally. But we can't all be perfect in our understanding. We are all growing in knowledge, so that means none of us knows it all yet. Since truth is infinite and we are finite, all of us have a long way to go—a lot to learn. That means we could well have errors in our understanding at any moment in time.

There are things we have heard since childhood that we have unconsciously added to the Word of God. There are also areas we are not aware of in the realm of truth, so in a sense we are taking away some truth. But this does not mean that we are heretics or apostates.

Pride is the sin behind true heresy and apostasy, which leads to deliberately adding to the truth of God's Word or taking some of it away. We must be on our guard against this and seek instead to communicate in the spirit of truth, being led by the Holy Spirit who has been given to guide us into all truth.

I heard a Baptist minister on a cassette tape once, speaking about this. He told how God called him to minister among Catholics in South America. He protested, "But God, how can I work with them? I don't agree with all they do and believe!" He said that God replied to him, "I work with you and I don't agree with all you do and believe, either!"

A greater degree of humility is needed within the body of Christ if we are ever to move together in the spirit of unity and cooperate in the task of world evangelism. Each one of us needs to realize, "I don't have exhaustive truth. I don't understand all things."

You see, God could not entrust all truth to any one person or group or denomination. Even the Bible had to come forth from many writers over a long period of time and from a wide geographic area. Today, God has given pieces of the puzzle of Bible interpretation to many different teachers and groups. Only as we fit the pieces together, humbly admitting that we have something to learn from one another, will we begin to see the larger picture. I don't believe any of us will see the big picture in its entirety this side of heaven. So, what do we do in the meantime?

Dr. D. G. Barnhouse was a respected Presbyterian theologian and the editor of "Revelation," the precursor to "Eternity" magazine. Even though he had taught that Pentecostals were in error, he accepted an invitation late in his life to spend a week ministering among Pentecostals. Later he said, "I found that ninety-five percent of what they believe, I believe. Two percent was totally contradictory and three percent was in a hazy area. I decided that I could set aside my differences of five percent for any brother or sister in the Lord."

The Word of God in Ephesians 4 tells us we need to be diligent to preserve the unity of the Spirit until someday we all attain to the unity of the faith (verses 2-13). We must agree on the basics—the divinity and Lordship of Christ, the Bible as the Word of God, the work of the cross, and other main tenets of the faith. But where we disagree, we must leave it to God and keep our hearts right. Our responsibility is to do everything we can to maintain the spirit of unity—the very spirit of Jesus (John 17).

Did Jesus say, "By this shall all men know that you are my disciples, because you have the same statement of doctrine"? No, He said they would know we belonged to Him because of our love for one another. You may be a pre-tribulationist or an amillenialist, a dispensationalist or a Charismatic, a Calvinist or an Arminian, but we can have fellowship in Jesus while the blood of Jesus is cleansing us from our sin.

If your doctrinal statement is separating you from other followers of Jesus, I would go so far as to say it has become an idol that must fall. After all, any doctrinal statement is only man-made, unless you do like Brother Andrew, the author of *God's Smuggler,* does. When anyone writes him and asks him for a doctrinal statement, he mails them back a Bible!

We need one another, in very real ways. It goes beyond an attitude of heart. We need to pursue cooperation in practical ways if the body of Christ is going to fulfill the Great Commission. We must communicate and complement one another wherever possible, doing away with duplication of effort.

We have a huge job to do, so we must find a flight pattern which doesn't collide with others in God's scheme of things. God's Spirit is being poured out on many people from diverse backgrounds, who are not being united organizationally, but simply in Jesus. This is His process of blending. If you're part of what He is doing today, you may have to give up some rights to doing things your way and the wrong of judging others. *You may have to surrender the right to prove that you're right.*

During World War II, thousands of Christians suffered in Hitler's prisons and concentration camps. One was a German named Martin Nieomuller. He was in solitary confinement, but one Christmas Day he was brought out of his cell and thrown in with three other Christian prisoners. One was from the Salvation Army, one was a Pentecostal, one was a Methodist and Nieomuller himself was from the German Free Evangelical Church.

The men found a discarded burnt door from a bombing, which they placed on the floor for a table. Using the black bread from their daily rations and some water, they celebrated the Lord's Supper together. Nieomuller reported, "As we knelt together on that cold stone floor, our theological differences vanished."

The body of Christ is not a prison. It is a fellowship of those who have found true liberty in Jesus Christ. As we walk in that liberty, we will find that He calls us to leave behind even the good things He has given us in order to find something greater—servanthood to His Great

Commission and unity with others who are different, but love Him as we do.

Is He calling you, right now, to walk in this kind of liberty?

CHAPTER SIX

Of No Reputation

Perhaps it was his Scottish burr, or the solid way he planted himself behind the lectern and declared the Word of God to us. But the vivid memory of Duncan Campbell as he spoke at our Youth With A Mission schools year after year, will always live in my mind, though he went to be with Jesus in 1974. Rev. Campbell was a Church of Scotland minister who had witnessed firsthand a revival of New Testament proportions in the islands of the Hebrides in Scotland in the 1950s. He told us stories of the supernatural and far from normal dealings of God with people he had seen, stirring in us the desire to see revival in our times.

One statement still rings in my mind, as it did the first time I heard that silver-haired man of God declare it: "I want to be known in Heaven and feared in Hell."

Many of us would be moved deeply by that statement. But are we willing to lay aside one of the most precious gifts of God—our reputation—in order to make it true in our own life?

Reputation is one of the most valuable things we own. Recently, a former White House aide was cleared of all charges after a long and costly court battle. He held a press conference and asked, "Will someone tell me, now. Where do I go to get my reputation back?" Usually, our reputation is something we take for granted until it is lost. Then we come to understand the words of Proverbs 22:1, "A good name is to be chosen rather than great riches."

The paradox is, if we want to be "known in Heaven and feared in Hell," we must be willing to lose our reputation here on earth. Jesus made Himself of no reputation when He came to earth (Philippians 2:7 KJV). He took the slurs and slanders of men in order to do God's will. Men and women in the Bible suffered loss of reputation to obey God. Put yourself in Noah's shoes, or in Jeremiah's, or Mary's, or Paul's. These were not popular people in their time.

Every great man or woman of God who left their mark on the pages of history faced the scorn and slander of their day. One was John Wesley. He and his brother, Charles, and George Whitefield are credited by modern historians for preventing a bloody revolution in England. Wesley's preaching brought hope to the oppressed in England's streets and alleyways. Yet clergy of his day called him a heretic, sometimes locking him out of their churches. Rumors were passed, charging him with every known sin. Pamphlets and books against him were circulated by leading churchmen and people high up in government and society. Many times he narrowly missed being killed by mobs stirred up against him.

Wesley accepted this as the norm, proof that he was obeying God in his ministry. One day Wesley was riding his horse along a road when it occurred to him that three whole days had passed without any persecution. Not even a brick or an egg had been thrown at him for three days! He was alarmed. He stopped his horse and fell down on his knees exclaiming, "Can it be that I have sinned, and am backslidden?"

He prayed, asking God to show him if he had done something wrong.

A rough fellow on the other side of the hedge, hearing the prayer, looked across and recognized Wesley. "I'll fix that Methodist preacher," he said and picked up a brick and hurled it at him. It barely missed him, but Wesley jumped up shouting, "Thank God, it's all right! I still have His presence."

How long has it been since anyone threw a brick at you? If everyone likes you, are you sure you are following Christ?

I know of no modern man or woman of God today with an effective ministry who did not first go through the pain of losing human reputation. I've had the privilege of knowing several major Christian leaders personally and they've all had the pain of being misunderstood, held up to ridicule, even defamed in the press or by clergymen.

Corrie ten Boom, an elderly Dutch lady who had gone to a Nazi concentration camp for her involvement in rescuing European Jews, was a friend who often spoke at our schools. One day, after the release of her popular book, *The Hiding Place,* and the movie based on it, I remarked to her, "Auntie Corrie, isn't it fabulous what God has done through your movie and book?"

She nodded her head and softly answered, "Loren, it is. But every day I remind myself I am prisoner number 66730." That was her number while she was a captive in Ravensbruck concentration camp.

Corrie had passed the test. She had been willing to be made of no reputation as she stood naked before the SS guards, waiting her turn in the showers. She related how she had stood there, a single lady in her late forties, suffering their cruel, mocking stares. Then the Lord reminded her that He, too, had been naked before men as He hung on the cross for everyone to see. And all who looked on Him despised Him. He gave up all reputation to save us.

This isn't to say you should seek to lose your reputation. You can lose your reputation by robbing a bank, but that's not what we're talking about. If you do what is right, accepting full responsibility for your actions and fully obeying the will of God, you will go through times when men do not understand and you lose your reputation. The wonderful thing about that is, your only reputation then will be His reputation.

When David Livingstone went to Africa as a missionary in the last century, he left behind a good future in Scotland as a doctor. His brother chided him, saying, "You can bury your life in the jungles among the heathen if you want to. I'm going to stay here in Britain and make a name for myself!"

His brother became a noted doctor of his time, but today his reputation is only one line in the Encyclopedia Britannica. He is mentioned as the brother of the famous missionary, David Livingstone, whose story fills fourteen paragraphs. When David died, he requested that his heart be buried in Africa. But the rest of his body was returned to Britain, given a royal funeral and buried by the High Altar in Westminster Abbey.

There may be things other than reputation that the Lord asks you to forego—things that people might call you insane or irrational for doing.

A number of years ago, the Lord challenged me to stop using my alarm clock and let Him wake me up at whatever hour He chose to speak to me. This went on for many months and even now, I sometimes find myself wide awake at a very early hour with great expectancy, knowing that God is wanting my fellowship. This isn't a hardship. It's a privilege.

There have been other times, alone or in a group, when God has said to spend the whole night in prayer. God knows we need sleep and this isn't some form of asceticism that we're talking about. But the Lord who created our bodies, the God who invented sleep in the first place can be trusted to make up to us any sleep we lose when we spend time with Him.

We give up the right to food for a period of time when the Lord directs us to fast and pray. Remember, Jesus told His disciples, "*when* you fast, do not be as the Pharisees...."

He said *when*, not *if*. Fasting is for all His disciples, whenever He directs, though others might view these actions as unreasonable.

The key to all of this is to avoid drudgery and legalism and obey the Lord with joy, finding excitement and fulfillment in being with Him and doing what He tells you to do. For thousands of years, so-called holy men have been trying to please or appease God by giving up pleasures, whipping themselves, lying on beds of nails, even limiting the number of breaths they took!

Imagine if we faced marriage the way some face their relationship with God. We would wake up and remember we were married and say, "Oh no, another day and I have a wife. I have to kiss her and be nice to her again."

But that's not the right attitude at all. The joy of loving your wife or husband makes the duties you do for her or him a pleasure. For Christians, there is a delight in being in God's presence that more than compensates for any right you give up to Him.

Another right that seems so basic, especially to Christians in the West, like me, is the right to be *free.* Every person has the right to freedom. Most of us from western countries have never known the experience of losing our freedom, but it is a right that we need to give back to God. The only real freedom we have anyway is in obeying Him. This statement would seem lunatic to anyone who does not know the joy of giving up rights to God, even when it puts you in danger.

It was twenty-five years ago in a Moslem nation of Asia. I looked around the hot, crowded gymnasium, filled with two hundred and fifty intelligent, enthusiastic Christian students. If we did what I was about to propose, every one of us could be in jail by nightfall.

A few fans on the wall were pushing the warm, humid air. I opened my Bible to Mark 16:15 and plunged in.

"It's against the law here in your country to witness to Moslems. The penalty is five years in prison, plus a $25,000 fine. But I believe when God tell us to go to every creature with the gospel, He means just that."

I looked down at Darlene, seated on the front row. Beside her sat a handful of foreign missionaries. We had only been married two months. For one quick second I imagined her in a tiny Asian prison cell. Could I do it? It was very quiet in the hot room.

"Stand up if you're willing to go out this afternoon and witness about Jesus to everyone you meet on the streets of this city—even if it means going to prison!"

I saw the faces turn to smiles, the eager light in several eyes. Then everyone stood, including the foreign missionaries! I reminded them of the risk, but everyone marched out and boarded the buses we had parked outside. Then we divided into pairs and scattered through the city, carrying our Bibles and tracts.

I don't recommend this in a closed country unless God tells you to do it, but we went to everyone we met, including the Moslems, whom we identified by their distinctive headgear. It seemed we all shared a certain recklessness, doing what we felt God was telling us to do.

The teams returned to share stories of what had happened. We saw many come to know Jesus Christ personally. The amazing thing we discovered was that our message and the conviction of the Holy Spirit were our protection from arrest. One pair of youth told how they had unknowingly witnessed to a secret policeman, on the job to report any attempts at proselytizing. He finally told them who he was after they had finished sharing. But he didn't arrest them. The youth reported that he seemed too impressed with the gospel to turn them in as he should have.

That was 1963. Since then we have had thousands of young people go into countries such as the Soviet Union, Mongolia and the People's Republic of China, boldly sharing their faith. Some have been arrested, and then released. A young African YWAMer named Salu Daka Ndebele was imprisoned for eighteen months in Mozambique, after the Marxist takeover in 1975. Salu told us from prison to send him all our newsletters and prayer requests, because he was spending his time in prayer for all of us!

As I write this book, a few of our workers are facing trial and perhaps several years' imprisonment in Nepal for their Christian faith. One girl named Kindra Bryan from Houston, Texas, was recently released after being held captive for three and a half months by guerrilla soldiers in Africa. Another of our workers from Switzerland has been taken hostage twice by militia factions in Lebanon.

I believe the reason North Korea, Tibet, Mongolia, Afghanistan, Saudi Arabia and other parts of the world are not evangelized is that we have been unwilling to surrender to Jesus our right to freedom. Brother Andrew says, "There is no country on earth closed to the gospel—as long as you're willing to go in and not come out again!"

Paul surrendered this right, and much of the New Testament is the result of his imprisonment. Paul made himself a slave of Jesus, and whether he was outside prison or inside, he was a truly free man. No one could take that away from him. He was chained at one time to two guards. Brother Andrew again comments that Paul must have prayed, "Thank you Lord for giving me a congregation that won't leave at twelve o'clock!" So Paul preached to his guards until their shift was over and he got another audience of two. Who was the prisoner?

Lots of times we hear people talking about one-third of the world being "closed to the gospel." Where did this term come from? Who closed that third? Is it God's idea? Did He say to go into all the world that is politically free and where it is legal to preach and give the gospel to every creature? No. The truth is, only the devil wants to close countries. If he can get you to believe a country is closed, then for you it is closed. But if we give up our right to freedom we can go anywhere on earth today.

Some of the greatest evangelistic exploits of our time are happening and most people in the West don't even know about them. But they are known and recorded in Heaven, and some day we will hear all the stories too. I met a Russian-born pastor named Earl Poysti who ministered on religious broadcasts into the Soviet Union for years. A visitor into the Soviet Union brought out this remarkable story to him.

A pastor had been put into prison fourteen years eariler for preaching the gospel. When he arrived, he decided God had given him this prison as a mission field. He began to look around for the worst criminal he could find in that institution. (Soviet prisons combine political and religious offenders with common thieves and others.) The man he settled on with his prayer and witnessing efforts was a murderer, a man who was so vicious that even the prison guards feared him.

In the prison, everyone was required to work for twelve hours a day, but the Christian decided this murderer would only be reached if he fasted and prayed for him. So he gave up the meager prison food, even though he continued his hard labor. When others sank into exhausted sleep, the pastor climbed out of his bunk onto the bare wooden floor to pray for the man's salvation.

One night while he was on his knees praying and shedding tears, he sensed someone behind him. He turned.

The murderer was staring him in the face. "What are you doing, man?"

"I'm praying," he replied.

"What are you praying for?" he asked gruffly.

"I'm praying for you," the pastor answered, wiping away his tears.

Soon that man gave his heart to the Lord. The change in him was so drastic that news of what had happened spread through the prison. The head of the prison called the pastor in to ask what he had done to this man.

"I didn't do anything," he answered. "I just prayed for him. It was God who changed him."

The prison boss said, "There is no God. What did you do?"

The Christian repeated what he had said. "Well, I don't like this stuff about God," the prison official said, "but I like the changes I've seen. I'm going to give you a lighter job in the kitchen so you can have more time to do to others what you did to him."

This was known as the second worst prison in the entire Soviet Union, but after some time, more and more came to know Jesus and a real change took place in the overall atmosphere of the place.

The pastor was transferred to the worst prison in Russia, with the promise that if he could bring a change there, they would give him an early release.

A move of God started at the second prison, leading the pastor to write his wife a painful letter. He begged for her to understand his decision. He was turning down his parole in order to continue his ministry in that prison.

This man had obviously given God his right to freedom and exchanged it for the privilege of seeing the Lord use him in a remarkable way.

I have heard it said, *Christianity that costs nothing is worth nothing.* Conversely, Jesus promised that anyone who obeyed His commands would be loved by the Father and would see great miracles in his life—along with persecutions and hardships.

In Youth With A Mission, we went for sixteen years without seeing one life lost, even though we had thousands of young people going out in sometimes perilous conditions.

Analee and Maria, two Finnish girls, were living in a Zambian village, sleeping on their bedrolls, lying on a straw covered dirt floor. Each night for a week, one would say to the other, "Don't you hear something?" The second girl reassured the first, and they went to sleep. At the end of the week, they decided to clean out the hut. Under the straw, directly beneath their bedrolls, they found a nest of cobras.

Several times, YWAMers were in potentially deadly car accidents, sometimes rolling vehicles, yet each time everyone was uninjured. On Long Island in the Bahamas, the brakes of a bus failed and it went out of control. The bus headed off the road, plunging through some underbrush toward a large tree. It stopped abruptly, inches from impact. The young people got out and looked underneath—heavy vines had wound themselves around the axle as they plunged through the bushes. This had gripped them just before their bus slammed into the tree.

Medical emergencies arose during those years, yet each time a doctor was found just in time or a pilot just happened to land in a deserted area who could evacuate the stricken one. Workers were arrested and imprisoned, yet from 1960 until 1976, no one died. With the thousands who served, statistics would show that some would die of natural causes or accidents. Yet no one did. We seemed to be living charmed lives.

Then in 1976, the Lord spoke to me. He told me He had been extending unusual protection during the foundational years of our mission, but now we would begin to see a number of deaths. Eventually, we would also see those who would die as a direct result of their Christian witness, as martyrs.

I gave this message to 1,600 of our workers at the Olympic Games Outreach in Montreal in July of that year. Within six months, we had our first two fatalities in the mission. They weren't the last. Three of our missionaries were murdered in the Philippines, and others have died of tropical diseases in Africa. The pain of calling parents and loved ones, telling them their precious daughter, son, father or mother has died is something that will never be lessened.

The Lord has not promised that there will be no fatalities in His army. He told the disciples as He sent them out that they would suffer death for His sake and for the gospel. Jesus said there is no greater love than a man lay down his life for another. He also promised that lives which fall, like seeds dropping to the earth, will produce a harvest in others one hundred times as great as if they had lived.

There have been more martyrs for the gospel in this century than in all previous centuries combined, according to Dr. David Barrett. This world missions expert has stated that an average of 330,000 Christians a year are being martyred for their faith around the world. Although ninety-five percent of these situations go unreported in the secular media, Barrett's investigations have found that one evangelist, pastor and missionary in every two hundred is being killed on the mission field and things are likely to get "even worse with the passage of time."

There will be more. The gospel must be preached in every nation and then the end will come, but we will see more martyrs and more danger as we evangelize in politically hostile lands, in countries torn by war and disease, and in Moslem nations and others virulently opposed to the Lordship of Jesus Christ.

Reona Peterson and Evey Muggleton were two young women who were willing to obey the Lord, even if it meant laying down their lives. Reona was a schoolteacher from New Zealand and Evey was a midwife from England. They got to know one another at our outreach center in Switzerland, where they joined my wife, Darlene, and four others who were especially interested in praying for the country of Albania.

You see, Albania was considered one of the hardest countries to penetrate with the gospel. It was the only nation that had stated that it was totally atheistic—including all of its people. The Albanian government claimed to have completely stamped out all religion. The authorities closed every church and mosque and killed those who would not renounce a belief in God. Some Christians met their death in 1969 by being sealed alive into barrels and rolled into the Adriatic Sea.

After months of prayer for this country, Reona and Evey believed God was leading them to go there themselves. They joined the only tour group available, made up primarily of Marxist youth from western Europe. The two women taped Gospels of John in the Albanian language underneath their clothes to get them in. Once inside the country, they prayed carefully before giving each piece of literature to individuals secretly, or laying copies in places where they could be found.

Reona and Evey were caught and brought separately before a group of interrogators. These men were well-trained in bringing fear to their captives, but each woman felt only peace and love from God as the Communists threatened them with prison and finally, the firing squad. Instead of quailing before them, both women were filled with boldness and witnessed to their captors about God.

The authorities promised them they would die at nine o'clock in the morning for crimes against the State of Albania, and they were led to their rooms. Reona said later that she was amazed to find how the grace of God prepared martyrs—her heart was full of peace and joy as she lay down for what she thought was her last night on earth.

In the morning, they were inexplicably released, dumped at the border without return tickets, money or passports. Through a series of amazing events, they found their way back to Switzerland. The full story is told in Reona's book, *Tomorrow You Die.*

It was a happy ending, but Reona and Evey were prepared to give their most precious right to Jesus, in exchange for the privilege of shedding His light in an incredibly darkened land.

Two who were not rescued were Mike and Janice Shelling. Mike was a New Zealander and Janice was from Minnesota. They had fallen in love and gotten married while working on one of our teams in the Philippines.

Mike and Janice lived in the mountains of the Philippines with their two-year-old daughter and three-month-old son. They were heading an effort to reach an unevangelized tribe nearby.

One night, Mike and Janice were murdered in their home. Fellow missionaries found their bloodied bodies the next morning. Their three-month-old baby lay unharmed in his crib upstairs, and the two-year-old girl was asleep on the dead body of her mother, whom she had apparently found that morning. Their murder was unsolved, but evidence pointed to the possibility that they were killed by one of the tribesmen they were trying to evangelize.

I was in New Zealand when I learned of our losing Mike and Janice. It seemed crushing to me—I couldn't forget the mental picture of that little toddler finding her mother's body and curling up on top of it to go to sleep. I cried out to the Lord. He had told me nine years before that our mission had been under an unusual protection and that it would be lifted.

"Is all your protection gone now, God?" I cried.

A few days later, there was a dramatic answer. Seven of our medical workers were in a van, on their way to their ministry post along the Cambodian border in Thailand. All of a sudden, black-clad guerrillas jumped out onto the road and began firing at them with automatic weapons, spraying their van with bullets. Evidently, they mistook the team for some of the factions fighting in the border area.

Our workers dived to the floor of the van while every window shattered and gunfire riddled the frame. Bullets quite literally went zinging past each one. Yet when it was over and they crawled out of the destroyed van, only one of them had been injured—a bullet had slightly grazed his head. They looked in amazement at their vehicle. Every seat was cut to ribbons by the gunfire, and the engine of the van was ruined, yet they were unharmed. When I heard of this, it was like God telling me, "You see, Loren, YWAMers are still under my protection."

The great faith chapter in the Bible is Hebrews 11. It tells us of those who had faith for life, faith for the parting of the Red Sea, faith to forsake riches, faith to bring down the walls of Jericho and shut the mouths of lions. Others with great faith faced death, being stoned, sawn in two, impaled by swords, exiled in the desert, being afflicted and destitute. There was no difference in their faith. Some, by faith, were rescued. Others, by faith, were killed.

Jesus, the originator of this faith, endured the cross and death for the greater joy that was in front of Him. His eyes were on His reward. Stephen, the first martyr, didn't die crying out in pain. He died with great joy and excitement as the heavens were parted for him and he saw Jesus, standing at the right hand of God the Father. The Word of God tells us that Jesus is normally *seated* at the right hand of His Father. But Jesus *stood* to receive Stephen!

If God asks us to give our lives to spread His word, we will see the tremendous blessings He has reserved for those who give up the greatest gift of all.

CHAPTER SEVEN

I've Got a Right to Be Mad

He was nineteen years old—but he couldn't remember anything before the age of sixteen. He had come up for counsel after I had spoken to a group of Christian campers in New Zealand. As we sat together on a wooden bench in the concrete building, praying together, God gave me a mental picture that I described to him. I saw a horse standing by a barbed wire fence.

That image triggered something in him. He said, "Yes, I remember!" Then he went on to relate the painful incident.

The boy had been hurt by a rusty barbed wire on a farm when he was twelve years old. The infection became so severe that he was hospitalized and finally, given up to die. Now as we sat on the hard bench in the campground, he sobbed as memories came flooding back.

He remembered his stepfather standing in the doorway of the hospital room and his mother saying, "Come in. He's about to die. Come say goodbye."

The stepfather's lip curled. "I don't want to see that dirty _______!"

The boy stopped his account, dropping his head. "He called me that name again. They always called me that name." The boy was illegitimate.

One story after another poured out as the hurtful memories returned. His own mother had tried to seduce him before he was fourteen. It was the joke of the family when his older brothers' girlfriends made sexual advances toward him. I saw how gracious God is to allow us the mechanism to forget—to blot out some of those deep wounds until the time when they can be healed. It hurt this young man terribly to share, yet as he related the story, he chose to forgive his parents and his older brothers. After our time together, he wrote to his parents and told them he loved them and had found God. He also wrote to his brother, now in prison for a rape conviction. I learned later that they wrote back, wanting to know more. They, too, were starving for this kind of love.

God is wanting to start a chain reaction of forgiveness around the world. Forgiveness is God's healing agent—without it we cannot be healed nor can others. But with forgiveness there can be dominoes of love falling around the globe, bringing real revival.

When Jesus taught His disciples how to pray, He said, "Forgive us our trespasses as we forgive those who trespass against us." God forgives us as we forgive others. In Matthew 6:14-15, He went on to say, "For if you forgive men their trespasses, your heavenly Father also will forgive you; but if you do not forgive men their trespasses, neither will your Father forgive your trespasses."

If you don't forgive, you shut off God's forgiveness. And it's His forgiveness that is holding the world together. Sin and selfishness are rampant on earth. Unless there is forgiveness, the world will blow apart at the seams.

When Corrie ten Boom got out of the concentration camp in Germany where she was held during World War II, she told God she would go anywhere to work for Him—except Germany! The Lord asked her to go to Germany—not only for her own healing, but for a healing of the German people.

After Corrie spoke in an auditorium there one day, a man came up to the platform. He had been a guard at one of the prison camps. He asked Corrie for her forgiveness. She stood there, praying silently, *God, I can't forgive him! He and the others are responsible for my sister's death!* The Lord said, *Forgive him for My sake.* She extended her hand, and at the moment when their hands clasped, she said a rush of forgiveness flowed through her. The feeling of forgiveness followed the act of her will.

Forgiveness is a choice. It is not optional for Christians, it is a command. God said, "I can't forgive you unless you forgive others." It is necessary for your mental, spiritual and even physical health. You must forgive.

Jesus came into the world not to condemn the world but that the world through Him might be saved. Romans 5:8 says that Christ extended His forgiveness while we were still sinners. On the cross, Jesus said, "Father, forgive them, for they know not what they do." He offered His forgiveness to the whole world. It is that love, that forgiveness God is asking us to give in order to lead men to repentance. World evangelism is dependent upon our forgiving.

In Paris, just prior to World War II, there lived a Frenchman of Italian extraction named Enrico. He was in the construction business. Not long after he came to know the Lord Jesus Christ as his personal Savior, he was out late one night, walking near his lumberyard.

Just then, he saw two shadowy figures jump out of a truck and make their way into his lumberyard. He paused and prayed.

"Lord, what should I do?" A plan came to his mind.

He walked over to the two men, who by now were already loading some of his lumber onto their truck. Quietly, he started helping them load the lumber.

After a few minutes, he asked them, "What are you going to use this lumber for?"

They told him and he pointed to a different pile of lumber. "That stuff over there will be better for your purposes," he explained.

When the truck was filled, one man said to Enrico, "You sure are a good thief!"

"Oh, but I'm not a thief," he replied.

"Yes, you are! You've been helping us out here in the middle of the night. You knew what we were doing."

"Yes, I knew what you were doing, but I am not a thief," he said. "You see, I'm not a thief because this is my lumberyard and this is my lumber."

The men became very frightened. The Christian replied, "Don't be afraid. I saw what you were doing but decided not to call the police. Evidently you just don't know how to live right yet, so I am going to teach you. You can have the lumber, but first I want you to hear what I have to say."

He had a captive audience! The men listened to him, and within three days both were converted. One became a pastor and the other a church elder. A load of lumber was a cheap price to pay for two souls, especially when you consider that Jesus taught us that one soul is worth more than the whole world.

It wasn't just the gift of lumber that led those two men to Christ—it was his act of forgiveness, extended when they were caught in the act of stealing. They knew Enrico could have them arrested and they knew that instead, this man was forgiving them, even before they repented. It was like Jesus on the cross, extending forgiveness to us before we repented.

The next step of forgiveness cost Enrico much more than a load of lumber.

It happened after the Nazis invaded and took over France. A Jewish family came to his door one night and he took them in, hiding them from the Gestapo for two years. Finally, someone discovered his secret and reported him. The Gestapo came and took the Jewish family away and arrested Enrico, as well.

Christmas Day, 1944, many months after his arrest, found Enrico in prison. The camp commandant called him in to see a beautiful meal spread out. He said, "I want you to see the Christmas dinner your wife sent for you before I eat it. Your wife is a good cook! She has sent you a meal every day that you've been in prison and I have enjoyed all of them."

The Christian brother was emaciated, the skin hanging on his frame and his eyes hollow with hunger. But he looked across the food-laden table and said, "I know my wife is a good cook. I trust that you will enjoy your Christmas dinner."

The commandant asked him to repeat what he said. Enrico did, adding, "I hope that you enjoy it, because I love you."

The commandant bellowed, "Get him out of here! He's gone crazy!"

The war ended and Enrico was released. It took him two years to regain his health, but he did. And God also started to bless his business again.

He decided he wanted to take his wife back to the town where he was imprisoned, to give thanks to God for sparing his life.

When they arrived, they learned the former commandant was living in that same village. Again, God gave Enrico an idea for creative forgiveness. He remembered that the commandant had enjoyed his wife's cooking. They went shopping, found a place to cook, and shortly, they appeared at the commandant's door with two baskets of food.

They were invited in, and Enrico said, "You don't recognize me, do you?" It occurred to him how different he must look, now that he had put his weight back on.

The commandant shook his head.

Then Enrico reminded him, "On Christmas Day, in 1944, I was in your office. I told you that I loved you and you said that I was crazy."

The former commandant paled and shrank from him. The Christian said, "Don't be afraid! We didn't come to hurt you. I told you that day that I loved you, and I still do."

The commandant stood there in silence, staring.

"I wasn't crazy, I really meant it. And I want to show you I mean it now. The war is over. It's peacetime and my wife and I would like to sit down with you and your wife and share a meal together. Would you allow us this privilege?"

As they started to eat the bountiful meal which Enrico's wife had cooked, the commandant suddenly threw down his knife and fork.

"What are you trying to do to me?"

The Christian replied, "Nothing. We just want you to know that we love you. We forgive you."

"How can you?"

"We couldn't have, on our own," said Enrico, "But Jesus Christ taught us how to forgive." He shared more and before the man could continue his meal, he knelt to find Jesus as his own personal Savior.

John 20:18 records that God used Mary Magdalene—a former prostitute—to tell the apostles that Jesus had risen from the grave. The disciples would not have known nor understood the message of resurrection if they hadn't forgiven Mary's past. If they had held her sins against her, they would have missed the most marvelous message of all time—the resurrection of Jesus Christ from the dead.

The Bible says, in John 20:23, "If you forgive the sins of any, they are forgiven; if you retain the sins of any, they are retained." If you retain the sins of anyone, refusing to forgive them, you cannot know the resurrection power of Jesus in your life either.

Some time ago, I heard a very unusual story. A pastor in Montana told me that he found himself wide awake one night. He glanced over at his digital clock, which read 2:22 A.M. He felt the Lord speak to him and say, "You are holding bitterness. You are not forgiving."

He didn't know of anyone he hadn't forgiven, so he asked God who it was. The Lord said, "You haven't forgiven Hitler."

"But, Lord," the pastor said, "Hitler is dead!"

The Lord replied, "I know that, but he's not dead in your heart."

He was reminded of how many times he had mimicked Hitler, making a mockery of him. He realized it was a real bondage and was making him insensitive to God's Spirit and to others. The Lord showed him he had a hardness in his heart toward someone he had never even met.

He said, "All right, God, I choose to forgive Hitler."

Then the Lord showed him other public figures, still alive, whom he needed to forgive.

As I listened to this pastor's story, I became more and more uncomfortable. One name came to my mind, loud and clear. Mao Tse-tung. Because of his brutality, he had never been one of my favorite people. I knew I had to get away by myself and pray.

Mao was alive at the time. As I knelt, I thought of the millions of people—many who were Chinese Christians—whom this man had slaughtered. Yet I had to forgive him.

I told God aloud, "I forgive Mao Tse-tung." Then I prayed for his conversion.

I had prayed for Mao before, but my prayers had always lacked real conviction. Now as I really forgave him, I found I could weep and pray for Mao as if he were a dear member of my family who was lost without God.

The Bible says, "The effectual fervent prayer of a *righteous* man availeth much" (James 5:16b KJV). You cannot release the power of God through prayer if you don't have the heart of God.

In order to pray effectively, we must pray with God's Spirit with His heart attitude towards individuals and situations. Only when we pray with forgiving spirits will we see Jesus answer our prayers.

When I realized I had not applied this principle in my feelings toward Chairman Mao, I chose to forgive him—even for the killing of so many people. Then I learned that I could release faith in prayer for a man whom I had never met.

A while later, I happened to read the September 20, 1976 issue of *TIME* magazine. In it, Henry Kissinger told of his last meeting with Mao Tse-tung. Mr. Kissinger said Mao talked about God and his concern over the fact that he was about to meet Him. Mao dropped from public sight during the last months of his life and was not allowed to meet any more foreigners after Kissinger. I wonder if he met God and found the forgiveness he was searching for? Certainly there were many Christians praying for him, just as there were those in the first century who prayed for Saul of Tarsus, another persecutor.

Forgiveness is laying down your life psychologically for another. It is laying down your emotional rights. Forgiveness is a choice not to remember what someone has done against you.

There are many hindrances to forgiveness. The first is not choosing to forgive. We *can* choose to love our enemies; Jesus told us to. And love always includes extending forgiveness.

If God commands anything, it is possible to do it. When you choose to forgive, He will help you. As Corrie ten Boom reached out her hand to the prison guard, God's grace was released to help her actually enjoy and participate in the forgiveness.

Another hindrance to forgiveness is the failure to forgive yourself. You must be able to forgive yourself if you are to forgive others.

In Holland, a man was telling me about his elder brother. He was very concerned over his brother's harsh condemnation of anyone who had committed the sin of sexual immorality. He went around in public, wearing signs that told people to repent. And although he realized his wife had been involved in this sin and bore an illegitimate child, he married her anyway. Later, however, he turned on her. He hated her and kicked her out of the house. The same man disowned his daughter when he learned of an immoral involvement she had as an adult.

The concerned brother asked me what he could do to help him. I felt God gave me an unusual answer—a little shaft of illumination.

"Tell your brother to receive God's forgiveness for the immorality he committed in the past and then he'll be able to forgive others."

I had no way of knowing this to be true by any natural means, but I was convinced the man was hiding this sin. I never heard the outcome, but I hope he was able to find God's forgiveness. If we judge others, often we reveal our own hearts. Romans 2:1 says, "For in passing judgment upon him you condemn yourself, because you, the judge, are doing the very same things."

Another hindrance to forgiveness is jealousy. The prodigal son's return was not heralded with great joy by his brother, who was jealous.

Pride is a fourth hindrance to forgiveness. Sometimes pride is manifested in a low view of yourself rather than an exalted view. You may say, "That's humility! I just don't think much of myself." No, it is actually pride. The more humility a person has, the greater true self-worth he has.

Pride is choosing to be deceitful about who you really are. It destroys self-esteem, making you insecure, vulnerable—afraid of being found out. Truth, on the other hand, is the basis for security. It is not true to say, "I am worthless." You are made in the image of God! When you have God's view of your own self-worth, you can be secure and transparent with others. And you can forgive.

Still another hindrance to forgiveness is a lack of understanding God's character, especially His mercy. Some have trouble believing in God's mercy because they have not seen this quality in their earthly fathers. Ask God to give you a revelation of His mercy through the scriptures. God is merciful. He always has been and He always will be. One way to receive this revelation is to read Psalm 136 KJV aloud and insert your name after each verse. "...for his mercy endureth forever for [insert your name]."

A double-standard, expressed in vindictiveness, is a sixth attitude that will hinder you from forgiving. You will end up duplicating the sin of the person with whom you are trying to get even. It came to my attention that one of our staff members was dealing harshly with those serving under him, often correcting people in public. I determined to deal with this and stop the hurts he was causing.

One day, I was in a small group with him and he struck out in this particular way. Immediately, I corrected him—publicly. Then it dawned on me that I had duplicated the very harshness I was correcting! In order to restore the relationship, I had to confess the wrong done, *publicly,* and ask his forgiveness.

Fear is another big hindrance to forgiveness, especially fear of further hurts. A young lady in Europe said, "I can't forgive. The people who hurt me did it so deeply that if I forgive them, I'll get hurt again." Forgiveness is the very key to protecting yourself from future hurts. When you truly forgive, it is like a broken bone that is set in a cast to mend. If it were not straightened, that arm or leg would be permanently misshapen.

Our souls need to be straightened with forgiveness instead of being allowed to twist and harden with bitterness and hurts we hold onto. The act of forgiveness releases emotional healing, making you strong enough to withstand future hurts.

You may say, "But you don't understand how much I've been wronged. You've never been hurt like I have!" That may be true.

But there is One who has been hurt like you and yet remained forgiving through it all. I'd like to share this story:

> At the end of time, billions of people were scattered on a great plain before God's

throne. Some of the groups near the front talked heatedly, not cringing with shame but with belligerence.

"How can God judge us? How can He know about suffering?" snapped a joking brunette. She jerked back a sleeve to reveal a tattooed number from a Nazi concentration camp. "We endured terror, beatings, torture, death."

In another group, a black man lowered his collar. "What about this?" he demanded, showing an ugly rope burn. "Lynched for no crime but being black! We've suffocated in slave ships, been wrenched from loved ones, toiled till only death gave relief."

Far out across the plain were hundreds of such groups. Each one had a complaint against God for the evil and suffering being permitted in this world.

How lucky God was to live in Heaven, where all was sweetness and light, where there was no weeping, no fear, no hunger, no hatred. Indeed, what did God know about what man had been forced to endure in this world? "After all, God leads a pretty sheltered life," they said.

So each group sent out a leader, chosen because he had suffered the most. There was a Jew, a black, an untouchable from

India, an illegitimate, a person from Hiroshima and one from a Siberian slave camp. In the center of the plain, they consulted with each other. At last, they were ready to present their case.

It was rather simple: Before God would be qualified to be their judge, He must endure what they had endured. Their decision was that God should be sentenced to live on earth as a man.

But because He was God, they set certain safeguards to be sure He could not use His divine powers to help Himself:

Let Him be born a Jew.

Let the legitimacy of His birth be doubted so that none will know who is really His father.

Let Him champion a cause so just but so radical that it brought down upon Him the hate, condemnation and eliminating efforts of every major traditional and established religious authority.

Let Him try to describe what no man has ever seen, tasted, heard or smelled. Let Him try to communicate God to men.

Let him be betrayed by His dearest friends. Let him be indicted on false charges and

> tried before a prejudiced jury and convicted by a cowardly judge.
>
> Let Him see what it is to be terribly alone, completely abandoned by every living thing. Let Him be tortured, and let Him die the most humiliating death with common thieves.
>
> As each leader announced his portion of the sentence, loud murmurs of approval went up from the great throng of people.
>
> When the last had finished pronouncing sentence, there was a long silence. No one uttered another word. No one moved. For suddenly, all knew—God had already served His sentence.*

He is *touched* by the feelings of our infirmities. He *knows* what we have known in suffering. He was *tempted* in every way that we have been.

That is why Jesus can show us how to forgive and how to receive forgiveness.

* Reprinted from "Right On," by Christian Liberation, Berkeley, California.

CHAPTER EIGHT

How to Be "Super Lamb"

In reading the Sermon on the Mount, have you ever unconsciously passed over the words, "The meek will inherit the earth?" The idea of meekness is faintly repugnant to many. We would prefer a John Wayne Christianity, where the men are men and the women are strong and beautiful.

Why did Jesus single out meekness in His longest recorded sermon? Was He saying that some day the world would be handed over to a bunch of wimps? What does it mean to be meek?

First, realize that Jesus Christ was not a weakling. I have been to the Israeli wilderness and have felt the furnace-like wind and seen the rugged mountains He climbed while fasting and praying for forty days. He had to have been in top physical condition—a real athlete—to have done that.

Jesus, you will remember, was a carpenter, and most of his friends were fishermen. They were blue collar workers. Perhaps if Jesus had come in our time, He would have worn a hard hat and worked with cranes and earthmoving equipment, building high-rises.

Jesus wasn't a wimp, and He isn't calling for an army of wimps. When Jesus says the meek will inherit the earth, we must understand the Bible meaning of meekness. Meekness isn't weakness!

Meekness is the character trait of a strong person who is continually surrendering his or her rights to God. Jesus was the perfect example of meekness, for as He said, He did *nothing* except what His Father told Him to do. Jesus was meek when He took out a whip and drove the money-changers from the temple, just as He was meek when He stood before Pilate and refused to utter a word to save Himself.

When Jesus said that the meek would inherit the earth, He was telling us His master strategy for winning the war against Satan and demon forces on this earth. God is going to utterly defeat Satan, and He's going to do it with individuals who move in the *opposite spirit* to the forces of darkness. We are going to win the victory, but only as we discern what the devil is doing and do the opposite thing in the power of the Holy Spirit.

Let me explain what I mean.

A number of years ago, during the springtime, I was invited to a Midwestern city to meet with thirty-eight North American Christian leaders. We had been called together to try and settle an issue that was threatening the unity of the body of Christ. It was a strictly private meeting, with both sides of the dispute meeting for prayer and heated discussion that lasted for several days.

I had the rather unusual position of being nonaligned on the particular issue. One man remarked, "Loren, you're like a man who parachuted into a war and you don't know which side to shoot at!" It would have been funny if it hadn't been so tragically true. The meeting was more like two sides of a war attempting a truce.

One day, we began to pray and I found I couldn't do anything but cry. It seemed to be coming from deep inside me. Then I became aware that another man was crying in the same manner. Even as I wept uncontrollably, my mind seemed to tell me that the two of us were crying on behalf of the Holy Spirit—for His grief over this disunity, this fresh wounding of Jesus Christ and His body.

We began to have a time of intercessory prayer with all assembled there. We started with a time of making our hearts right before God. There was a time of silence, while each of us asked God to show us areas of sin to confess to Him. Some leaders confessed wrongs aloud to the group. Then we asked God what He wanted us to pray about.

A man on one side of the controversy said, "God has told me we are to pray for Jerusalem."

Then, from the other faction another said, "I confirm that. God spoke the same thing to me."

What happened next was most unusual. A third man spoke, saying, "God is showing me a mental picture. A vision. I see a wild boar tearing up a vineyard!"

What a strange thing, I thought. Yet another person said, with mounting excitement, "God brought a scripture reference to my mind. I looked it up and it was about a wild boar in a vineyard!" He read aloud the passage from Psalm 80 that held this unusual reference. Amazement began to dawn on faces around the room. Something far bigger than us was at work here.

We bowed our heads and one or two prayed, asking God to help us understand what the "wild boar" meant, and the "vineyard." It was such a curious scripture passage.

Then one of the men spoke up and said he had an idea: God was using the wild boar to symbolize a spirit of religious controversy, and the vineyard was Jerusalem.

It suddenly seemed clearer. The understanding was falling in place for all of us in that room. I know it made sense to me.

My mind flicked back to the occasions when I had visited the Holy Land. Jerusalem is the birthplace of three religions which have fought and shed one another's blood over centuries: Judaism, Islam and Christianity. I remembered the sense of outrage I felt at the display of religious disunity in Jerusalem, whose very name means "Peace." It was like a religious Disneyland. Every kind of religious practice, ritual, shrine and festival were there.

Even the various branches of Christianity vie for attention, each claiming to have the *true* sites of various happenings in the life of Christ. In one of these shrines, shared by different sects, a fist fight broke out once because a priest from one side lit the candles belonging to the other side!

In our meeting in the Midwest that day, after we understood the wild boar vision, we began to pray fervently for the peace of Jerusalem. We asked God to bring an end to the religious controversy that had torn the city for hundreds of years.

Then the man who had received the vision exclaimed, "I can still see the wild boar. It's looking directly at me and it's not moving!"

A chill crept around my neck. It was as if Satan were mocking us. We were powerless against him, no matter how earnestly we prayed.

At that moment, another leader spoke aloud with a word from the Lord: "You cannot drive out that spirit of religious controversy because you yourselves are not united!"

The meeting broke up after four and a half days. Not everyone left our meeting in peace and agreement, but God began a process there of public and private humbling. Many stood in those four and a half days to confess shortcomings and ask forgiveness for publishing charges against other Christian ministers, under the guise of defending doctrinal truth. As we left, the temperatures had cooled. We still didn't share the same ideas, but we shared a sense of love for one another. The controversy was defused.

For me, though, the experience was the loose tail of a ball of string that began to unravel, showing me why we were so often powerless before Satan. I slowly began to see how the principle of ministering in the opposite spirit really works.

Many Christians struggle with a sense of powerlessness over the darkness in their lives. Yet Jesus has given us, His followers, authority over all the power of the enemy, promising that we would win as we engaged Satan in battle. His Word states that the gates of Hell would not prevail against His Church. But we will have no power nor authority against the devil, either in prayer or evangelism, if we are not moving in the opposite spirit and attitude to him in any given situation.

When Jesus sent out seventy of his followers to go and minister ahead of him, He said, "I send you out as lambs in the midst of wolves." Ordinarily, wolves make short work of eating lambs. But not in this case.

God's master strategy for taking back the people of the earth from Satan's hold does not include our using excessive force—even though He is infinitely more powerful than the devil and has a force of angels that outnumbers Satan's, two to one. He is going to use lambs—meek ones, but not weak ones. Super lambs!

God isn't interested in shortcuts, either. Have you ever really thought about Jesus' temptation in the wilderness? What was the devil trying to get Him to do? I believe it was to take a shortcut, to avoid all the pain and humiliation of the cross by going after God's will the devil's way.

The devil promised to give Jesus all the kingdoms of the world if He would worship him. God's goal in sending Jesus to earth was to give His Son all the kingdoms of the world. One day, it is predicted in Revelation, the kingdoms of the earth will be the kingdom of our Lord (Revelation 11:15). In a smaller way, this kingdom is already coming through the Church of Jesus Christ. But someday it will be finally and completely fulfilled when Christ returns to earth.

Satan was promising Jesus the instant achievement of that goal, sidestepping the pain and suffering of the cross and the obedience of Christ's followers for many hundreds of years afterwards.

What do we learn from this story? Jesus refused Satan and we must refuse him, too. We have to learn to discern when the devil is offering us a shortcut—when he is tempting us to do God's will the devil's way.

Have you ever wondered why God doesn't go ahead and throw the devil into the bottomless pit now and do away with his evil influence and power? There are many answers to this question—perhaps an entire book's worth—but I want to concentrate on just three.

I believe God allows Satan's attacks, first of all, to destroy his works through our obedience. Satan comes in darkness, but our obedience to the Holy Spirit turns the light on. We often hear about the speed of light, but a friend of mine named Campbell McAlpine likes to talk about the speed of darkness. The darkness flees just ahead of light: about 186,000 miles per second. So just turn on the light!

A number of years ago, we were conducting training schools in a rented mansion in Hilo, on the eastern side of the island of Hawaii. The facility was ideal, large enough to house many of our students and with a living room suitable to be our lecture room and chapel.

We had a lease through the summer of that year, after which we planned to move to Kona, on the western side of the island. But one day we were approached by our landlord. Another group wanted the facility and was willing to pay for us to leave early. It wasn't that simple, though.

The group wanting to move in were bringing with them an evil mix of eastern religion, drugs and sexual immorality. They worshiped the man who was their guru. (Later, it was reported that they had killed a baby as a human sacrifice.) They were offering us $2,000, just to get us to move out two weeks early.

We prayed and asked God what to do. We had the perfect right to refuse them—our lease wasn't up yet. Instead, we had some rather surprising guidance. The Lord impressed us to go ahead and move out, and not to fight them. One scripture that was quickened to me was 2 Samuel 5. In this chapter, God told David and his armies not to move until they heard the sound of marching in the tops of the balsam trees, because He Himself was going out ahead of them to strike the army of the Philistines. It was the description of an ambush.

I sat and pondered this. Was God setting up some kind of ambush against this group? Is that why He wanted us to do nothing, and just move out?

The guru sent two young women, wearing sexually provocative clothes, to try and persuade us. Sitting on the lawn furniture behind the mansion, they again offered the $2,000. I told them kindly but firmly that we didn't want their money. We would move out immediately, but we wouldn't touch their money.

"But, why?" one asked. Apparently, they had been prepared for a fight, but not for this.

Ever since this situation had developed, we had been praying earnestly for the people in this group to be set free and come to know Jesus as their Savior. So now, sitting behind the mansion, I began to tell these two women about Jesus Christ, and how He was the only one they should worship and serve. I told them we would move out early—but only because God had told us to. Then I warned them of the spiritual deception they were caught up in. For $2,000, I had purchased an excellent chance to witness to these two women about Jesus.

We moved to Kona, but reports came to us of the wickedness going on in the Hilo mansion. They set up a throne in the very room where we had prayed and worshipped Jesus and heard lectures from the Word of God. They put the guru on that throne and bowed down to him. As we heard of this, my skin crawled and I remembered the strange idea that God was setting up an ambush.

In just eight weeks, the guru was hang-gliding on another island. A freak wind came up and blew him against jagged cliffs along the shore.

His followers brought his battered body back to the mansion, refusing to have him embalmed, believing for three days that his decomposing body would rise from the dead. He didn't. God had set up an ambush.

A few weeks later, I learned through Pat Boone that his neighbor's daughter, and at least one other who had been in that cult, had become converted and were now followers of Jesus. The cult itself disbanded. Still later, after our center was established in Kona, we returned to once again use the mansion in Hilo for a Christian training program. Darkness had fled before the light, and all we had to do was obey God, witness for Him and turn down $2,000.

God allows attacks from the enemy in order to extend Christ's Kingdom on earth. We take literal ground for God in this world every time we respond correctly to Satan's offensive. Perhaps the greatest illustration of this happened in the centuries following Christ's return to Heaven.

A tiny band of Christians found themselves pitted against the formidable forces of the entire Roman Empire. A giant nation with hundreds of thousands of soldiers, enslaving every known nation on earth, fueled by the ambition and greed of its citizens and the madness of its dictators, had turned its entire fury upon a handful of people who preached that the Son of God had come to live, die and rise again in a remote part of the empire.

Early believers responded to this onslaught in the opposite spirit. Thousands went meekly to their deaths in every terrifying form which successive emperors could devise. But the meek won the war. For every Christian torn apart by the lions of the arena, more would see their silent witness and join their ranks. Within three hundred years, Christianity became the official religion of Rome. Eventually the world's mightiest nation lay in ruins, while Christianity continued to spark and spread among new lands and peoples. The meek do inherit the earth.

A third reason God allows the enemy to attack us is so that He can provide for our needs through those attacks: spiritual, mental, emotional, material and physical.

When Samson was attacked by a lion, he destroyed the wild beast in the power of the Spirit. Later, he returned and found honey in the carcass of the animal. Samson gave this riddle to the Philistines: "Out of the eater came something to eat, and out of the strong came something sweet." What does this mean to us?

Satan comes against us as a roaring lion, seeking to devour us. But in every attack the Lord allows, there is a blessing in store for us. As we move in the opposite spirit, God causes the wicked to store up for the righteous! (Proverbs 13:22)

The book of Esther tells us that Satan stirred up a wicked, ambitious man against a good man. Haman's hatred and envy of Mordecai led him to plan Mordecai's murder. Instead Haman was hung on the gallows prepared for Mordecai, and his beautiful house and possessions were given to Mordecai. God allowed the wicked to store up for the righteous.

Jesus said we are to go out as lambs. When we come into a conflict with the world and respond the way worldly people do, fighting fire with fire, we stop being lambs and become wolves.

A friend of mine, Gary McKinney, who leads our ministry in Spain, was visiting with me and told me of an experience he had had.

Gary was visiting his parents in New York State when one day he saw two members of a cult group walking up to the front door. As they rang the doorbell, Gary asked the Lord what to do. God told him to share how much Jesus meant to him from his time of devotions that morning.

So Gary invited them in, and began to talk to them about Jesus. He refused to be drawn into an argument. He just told them how real Jesus was and what He had done for him that very week. They opened up to him. Instead of launching into their prepared arguments, they quietly listened to Gary and asked him questions.

As Gary related his story, my mind was elsewhere. With a strong stab of my conscience, I remembered an encounter I'd had with a member of that same worldwide cult. Only it was a very different story.

It was during a door-to-door witnessing outreach in Seattle. Each day, we had different partners as we went out two by two to talk to people about the Lord. That particular day, I was teamed with a pastor who was a good friend of mine. It would be a fun day, I thought.

We walked up the walkway to one particular house—just another suburban tract home—and were met at the door by a square, balding man in his thirties. To our surprise, there was none of the usual "sales resistance." He eagerly ushered us in, offered us a seat and settled back to talk.

My friend opened his Bible to begin, but first the man fired a question at us.

"What do you think about the Trinity?"

I shot a look at my partner. He gave me a little smile, for now we knew who we were dealing with. We asked him if he was in such and such a group, and he admitted proudly to being one of their local leaders.

We settled back and got into serious debate. No one was better prepared to disprove this cult's beliefs than my friend and I! We launched into a barrage of arguments with the man, and he parried, countering our scriptures with his scriptures, our logic with his own.

It was a great debate, and after an hour or two, I noticed the man was wilting. He was out-gunned. Finally, all his geniality disappeared. Angrily, he stood and asked us to leave.

My friend and I walked down the street with our Bibles, laughing and congratulating ourselves on how we had won over the well-honed argument skills of this cult leader.

Now, years later, I remembered that afternoon and dropped my head in shame. I'd thought I had won, but now I knew I had lost. The contrast between the story I had just heard from Gary—his gentle, loving reaction to the two in New York—and my own reaction in Seattle couldn't have been greater. I could hardly wait to finish my conversation with Gary, and get away by myself.

Alone, I prayed and asked God to forgive me. I had violated the principle of ministering in the opposite spirit. That particular cult is known by its aggressive, arguing spirit. It is controlled by the spirit of religious controversy. Instead of meeting that spirit with the opposite one, humility, I had entered into it and embraced the same spirit. We had won the argument that day in Seattle but had left behind a man who was humiliated and further alienated from the gospel.

There are many spirits or manifestations of the devil and his forces working around us. One of the spirits of Satan most rampant in the world today is the spirit of greed. Have you ever had an experience when greed seemed personified on human faces? I did. It was a number of years ago when we were trying to buy our property for our Christian university in Kona, Hawaii.

The property, a former hotel, had been entangled in bankruptcy proceedings for eight years. Several were fighting for the right to buy it. Squatters had moved into the disused hotel, and the caretaker was illegally renting to them. We heard about all sorts of unlawful activities going on at the property, which had rapidly become overgrown with dense tropical bush. In the buildings were drug trafficking and prostitution, and the local people hinted at political corruption in the situation.

Yet God was telling us to buy this particular place. We prayed and He even impressed us with the exact price we were to offer and the terms for payment.

On the day of the hearing, my lawyer and I were confident as we strode into the oak-paneled courtroom to make our offer. Dotted throughout the gallery were various parties waiting with their lawyers, also eager to buy the hotel.

The attorneys rose in turn to speak, each grasping after his client's share. I watched as the demands became more and more heated. Every party was demanding their rights. It reminded me of small children, each one tugging at the same toy. The spirit of greed was like a physical presence in the courtroom. Those who held the hotel in receivership were asking for a price more than four times the amount we were going to bid.

The judge behind the high, old-fashioned bench looked down at me. "Mr. Cunningham, I understand you have an offer to make."

We didn't have very much money at all, but we did have the word of the Lord. So I confidently made our bid to the judge—the exact amount which the Lord had impressed us. Somehow, we would get the rest.

I returned to Kona and called our group together to pray. I was sickened by the greed I had just seen, but were we in fact any different? Weren't we just as eager to buy this prime property as the others in that courtroom?

As objectively as possible, I made a mental checklist of our attitudes and the reasons we wanted to buy the hotel. Yes, we were different. We would not benefit personally from this property—we would merely use it to carry out God's work, and that would be done in a frugal, no-nonsense manner. And not only did we want it for different reasons, but we would get it in a very different way. We would move in the opposite way to greed. What is the opposite of greed but giving and generosity?

There were two hundred and fifty of our staff and students in Kona, where we were attempting to buy the hotel. We each turned our pockets inside out, giving money for a deposit on the property. We came up with $50,000, but it wasn't enough.

We had saved a large amount of money in our mission for the eventual purchase of a ship to carry practical aid and the Word of God to needy ports of the world. We had been praying and believing for that ship for a long time. But we decided God wanted us to give away the money—an amount in six figures to Operation Mobilization, another mission that was purchasing a ship for ministry.

After we did this, a third Christian ministry, Daystar, gave us some property worth ten times more than the amount we had given to Operation Mobilization. That property gave us collateral to apply for a bank loan. We were on our way to buying a hotel!

The days stretched into months as we continued the process of praying, giving, praising God for eventual victory, applying for bank loans and waiting to see if our bid would be accepted.

During this waiting period, the Lord showed us we were to have a time of generosity beyond cash offerings. We each asked God if there were something we owned that we should give to someone else. The purpose wasn't to get funds. It was simply an act of generosity to counter the spirit of greed operating in this situation.

For several days it continued, as individuals prayed, then went to their rooms and apartments and brought out their treasures. One family gave another a beautiful oil painting, others gave household items and favorite pieces of clothing. One boy gave away a surfboard for which he had saved for months, only to receive a pair of shoeskates from another kid. As we gave, it wasn't painful at all—it was fun! It felt like Christmas.

We saw the spirit of greed broken wide open in the spiritual realm in those months. Some may explain it away, saying we just got lucky. But all two hundred and fifty of us knew—it had been the simple act of giving that allowed us to finally purchase the property eleven months later at the exact price and terms which we had originally been given by the Lord—one-fourth the asking price of the owners.

There are many different spirits and corresponding attitudes in operation at any given time. A spirit is a personality, but it also influences our attitudes and conduct. The Holy Spirit is personal and so are Satan and his fallen angels. You can be under a spirit's influence, moving in the same attitude, or you can move further and actually become possessed by that spirit. But even if you are only fleetingly influenced, for an hour or a day, you can never win spiritually for God until you are free from that spirit and moving in the opposite way—Christ's way.

There is, for example, the spirit of disloyalty. We must move in loyalty. We must be committed to the cause of Christ more than we are committed to examining our personal differences in the body of Christ. We've had enough walls built in the body of Christ. It's time for bridges! In an age when people are so apt to attack others' actions, beliefs and motives, in a day when Christians address other Christians' faults over the national media, it's time to return to loyalty. Not blind loyalty, but loyalty that includes forgiveness and a commitment to work together over faults and differences, to go in private to settle wrongs (Matthew 18:15). Love covers a multitude of sins. We need to restore each other in gentleness (Galatians 6:1).

Satan is also moving in the spirit of independence. He wants us to think that we, and the particular group we belong to, can stand alone. Peter Marshall and David Manuel, in their book, *The Light and the Glory*, describe how the Pilgrims came to the land of America. They entered into covenant relationships with one another for the purpose of winning the Indians on this continent to Christ and establishing a missionary nation to reach the world. At first, they continued in that spirit, each one committed to the other, and began to see great numbers of Indians turning to the Lord Jesus Christ.

Then the spirit of independence was introduced. Each colonist received three hundred acres of land for himself. They began to seek personal wealth rather than the common purpose they had before. After that, Indian uprisings began, and the peace between the white man and the Indian was shattered. The resultant slaughter and bloodshed lasted more than two centuries, and America strayed very far from that missionary purpose of the first settlers.

Today, we Americans still continue to have more than our share of pride and independence. It is the source of some denominations in this country being splintered into scores of different organizations, each one saying, "We can't learn from others. We've got it all ourselves. We don't need anyone else." That is the spirit of independence and it can only be won over by a spirit of *interdependence*, recognizing our need of one another and committing ourselves to each other in humility and unity.

There is also the spirit of immorality. It must be met by the spirit of purity.

Back in the 1950s, the drug epidemic first became known to most Americans through the violence of juvenile delinquents in the inner-cities. Who did God raise up as a voice in this situation? A former drug addict? Someone well versed in the ways of the streets, in the laws of urban jungles? No. He brought a skinny, country preacher, totally ignorant of the complexities of sin he found in New York City.

David Wilkerson, who later wrote of his experiences in *The Cross and the Switchblade,* couldn't have been more opposite to the tough, street-hardened addicts to whom he brought the message of Christ. It was the principle of winning through the opposite spirit.

At one point, David was surrounded by armed gang members, threatening him with their switchblades. David responded, "You can cut me in pieces if you like, but every piece of me will still go on loving you!"

Right now, Satan is having a heyday with the spirit of rejection and alienation. Many have been wounded as children and still expect people's reaction to them to be rejection. Much of the sexual immorality so commonplace today is rooted in rejection. Men and women are looking for acceptance and affirmation through sexual immorality of all kinds.

We Christians agree that all have sinned, and that Jesus died for sinners and will forgive any who come to Him in repentance, confessing and forsaking their sins. But there is one sin that is harder for us to forgive than any other—one group of sinners that most Christians avoid above all others. That group is homosexuals. Some Christians even doubt that homosexuals can be saved and changed. It has become, for us, the unpardonable sin.

We may say that we hate the sin and love the sinner, but how many of us can walk up to a homosexual, put our arm around him and say we love him?

Anyone can detect a spirit of love, or pick up on a veneer of false love, covering an attitude of loathing.

I have come to the conclusion that the sin of homosexuality—and it is a sin—is not a condition you are born with, but a choice. It is a temptation to people who have been rejected. They have sought for love and are finding it in a counterfeit way, which is lust. In a cruel paradox, rejection leads them to homosexuality, which in turn brings them further rejection from society. And the counterfeit love of homosexuality becomes bondage. Homosexuality is a powerful bondage, but it will never be broken if we as Christians are not able to offer its victims the love and acceptance they were seeking in the first place.

Now, the spread of AIDS often considered a homosexual disease in the West, has fueled that massive rejection. One homosexual AIDS victim recently lay dying in a Dallas hospital. A volunteer was helping him write out his will when she noticed a tear rolling down the man's face. She reached over and put her arms around him and held him. After a minute, he spoke. "Do you know how long it's been since anyone touched me?"

As far as I know, it wasn't a Christian who was offering him that human warmth. It should have been. I believe this modern plague could offer the Church a tremendous opportunity to extend love and see thousands of homosexuals set free.

How many people, homosexual and heterosexual, do we turn away from the gospel because we try to hit them over the heads with our Bibles? They turn away, but perhaps they are not rejecting the gospel but our condemning approach. It is possible to move in the gentle spirit of truth, and still be able to show people the sin from which they must be set free.

There is a spirit of covering up, or concealment, based on pride. We need to meet this spirit with its opposite: transparency with God and with one another. Transparency is the fruit of humility. Humility is being willing to be known for who you are. Pride is trying to be known for something that you are not.

When the public demands that its political and religious leaders be open and honest with them, that is right. But we must also be open and honest with one another—pastors with their congregations; teachers with their students; parents with their children; leaders with their followers; followers with their leaders; husbands with their wives—everyone.

Why is it some people seem closer to God than others? Why do some struggle along in mediocrity while others seem to take off in the extent of their authority and ministry? We are all equal at the foot of the cross, but you can easily see that we are not all equal in the extent of the scope of our influence and ministry and power with God.

The larger your ministry, the greater degree of transparency and openness you must have. You see, the enemy can have power over us if there is any unconfessed sin in our lives. Perhaps we have a sin which we have confessed to God, but we live in fear that it will someday be brought out against us. The devil becomes our blackmailer, holding that secret over us.

Unconfessed sin is an area of weakness until we bring it out into the light. Once confessed and repented of, it is under the protection that openness with God and with man brings. Then if your enemies bring something against you, you can say, "That's already taken care of. I've confessed it to God and to the appropriate people." Childlike transparency was the key to the authority Jesus had when facing His accusers.

Fear is perhaps the greatest spirit we have to combat in ourselves and in the world as we go out to take ground for God. His Word teaches that perfect love casts out fear, so love is the opposite of fear.

I had a great, secret fear in my life as a young husband. It went on for years before I understood the basis of it and endeavored to deal with it.

Darlene is the most precious person to me in this world. As I told you in the first chapter, I gave up my rights to her life when we were involved in a car accident in Arizona. But a strange string of events led to a deeper understanding. Sometimes we need to do more than relinquish rights—we need to understand what the enemy is trying to do in our lives and combat it in the opposite spirit.

Darlene was involved in a series of mishaps. When we were newlyweds on a ministry trip to Samoa, Darlene slipped and fell on the slippery edge of an ocean side cliff, with swirling waves below. She lay unconscious, where I found her, with her feet over the edge. We later learned that each year a few people slipped at that spot, fell into the ocean and were washed out to sea by powerful tides. In fact, we found out that the local name for the place was Sliding Rock.

Two years later, we were involved in the car accident in Arizona, which I told about in the first chapter. Again, Darlene was almost killed.

A year after that, she and I were driving two vehicles in convoy on the Pennsylvania Turnpike. We had been given a station wagon for our mission and were on our way back from picking it up. To my horror, I looked in my rearview mirror to see her car spinning out of control in the midst of several large trucks. Her vehicle hit the center divider on the turnpike and the gas tank burst into flames. Yet, somehow Darlene got out unharmed.

Sometime later, one winter while we were living in Switzerland, Darlene reached behind an industrial-size washing machine to retrieve a piece of laundry. She didn't know someone had been working on that machine and had left a protective cover off. Her hand touched a live electrical wire. She stood there with snow-covered shoes on a concrete floor, frozen to the exposed wires with her body pinned against the steel of the washer as 380 volts of electricity coursed through her body.

Darlene told me later that she screamed and screamed and no one heard her. She cried out to the Lord to save her life, but still the jolts pounded through her. "Lord," she finally cried, "we've given our lives to you and I'm praying and it's not working!"

Instantly, God spoke to her. "Bind the devil."

Darlene knew what that meant. She bound the devil, praying against him in the authority of Jesus Christ (Matthew 16:19). As soon as she did, she was hurled off the live wire and slammed into the wall opposite the washing machine. For several days she experienced heart palpitations and weakness and the hole burnt in the palm of her hand took months to heal. But she was all right. Again, though, it was Darlene who had almost been killed.

After a few years of these and other accidents, it occurred to me that something was going on. Maybe it wasn't just that Darlene was accident-prone. Perhaps this was a spiritual battle.

It is not enough to guess at things in the spiritual realm. We don't have to be ignorant of Satan's devices against us. I asked the Lord to give me understanding and He gave me a dream.

I was standing on a cliff, looking down on the rocks below, where I could just make out a body. People started to gather around the body and with a sudden feeling of desolation, I knew it was Darlene.

I woke up and tried to shake off the lingering fear, but it stayed. Then I prayed and it dawned on me. Darlene's life had been targeted by Satan—or perhaps the target was just me and my fear for her life. Strangely, I was aware that all this was connected somehow with my grandfather—my dad's father—and the tragedy that marred his life.

Grandpa Cunningham was a young minister with a growing popularity as he went from church to church, teaching and expounding the Word of God. He loved the Bible and spent every spare minute in it until he knew so much scripture by memory that they called him "The Walking Bible."

When my dad was five years old, Grandpa's lovely young wife died of smallpox. He stumbled into another marriage, trying to find someone to care for his five children while he attempted to continue his traveling ministry. The marriage was a disaster. There was a divorce and Grandpa spent the rest of his years preaching in small, backwater places. His promising career as a preacher was flawed, if not ended. Much other misery happened, which is told in greater detail in my book, *Is That Really You, God?*

As these details came to mind again, I saw what my dream meant and why so many things had been happening to Darlene. My grandfather's ministry had been attacked through the death of his wife, and now Satan was trying to attack me with fear that my wife, too, would die.

Once I recognized this, I commanded Satan in Jesus' Name to stop bringing these accidents on Darlene. I surrendered her again to God and asked the Lord to remove the fear from my heart. That was six years ago. The string of Dar's accidents ended.

You see, you can't be in fear for someone you have given to God. The opposite of fear is love, power and a sound mind (2 Timothy 1:7 KJV). As we move in these spirits opposite to fear, we can see God moving on our behalf in a powerful way. He can either release to us the strength to suffer, and even die for His name if necessary, or He can deliver us, protecting us supernaturally.

Such was the case with a little girl in East Germany. I heard her story from Pastor Gerhard Wessler, while speaking at his church in Frankfurt.

This little ten-year-old was the daughter of a Christian family in Mecklenburg, East Germany. She had to attend the local communist school where they systematically tried to destroy the students' belief in God.

For instance, the teacher would tell the children to bow their heads on their desks and ask God for candy. After waiting awhile to see that nothing happened, the teacher would laugh and say, "See, students, there is no God! Now, ask the government for candy." Then a piece of candy would be given to each on the government's behalf.

One day, the teacher told the students to stand and repeat after her, "There is no God."

The little Christian girl refused, explaining to her teacher, "But I believe there *is* a God." The teacher seized on this helpless little girl, determined to make her change.

"You are to write a paper tonight. Put this statement down fifty times: 'There is no God.'"

The little girl went home, prayed with her parents about the problem, then wrote fifty times, "There *is* a God!"

When she returned with this paper the next day, her teacher was enraged. The woman lashed out. "This time you will write, 'There *certainly* is no God' seventy times. And if you don't, you and your parents are going to be in a lot of trouble!"

The child and her parents prayed again and she returned with another paper, writing seventy times, "There certainly *is* a God!"

The teacher became furious when reading it, shouting, "For tomorrow, you write one hundred times, 'There *definitely* is no God!' And if you continue to resist, I'll go to the police and you and your parents will see what happens!"

By now this incident had become known in all the village. It was a fight between the powers of light and the powers of darkness. The parents of the little girl knew what was at stake. But they would rather suffer than deny their Lord. So the little girl wrote one hundred times: "There definitely *is* a God!"

The following day the teacher looked at the paper and with her voice shaking, she shouted: "Now I'll go and denounce you at the police office. Let's see whether your God will help you!"

At this, the teacher went out to the school yard, got on her bicycle and rode towards the road. But she didn't get far. When she passed the school gate, she suddenly fell from the bike—her heart had stopped and she lay dead on the ground.

The children saw this, having watched her through the classroom window. They ran out of the room and gathered in shock around her body. Then one person shouted out loud and the others joined in, chanting: "There definitely *is* a God! There definitely *is* a God!"

When we have relinquished our rights to God, we have nothing to fear from the enemy. Even a little girl who belongs to Jesus has more power than an entire atheistic government! God can either deliver us, or He can give us the strength to suffer for His Name.

As we move in the opposite spirit, we can indeed be the meek who inherit the earth.

CHAPTER NINE

Winning It All

When I am speaking to a group and challenge them from a popular Bible verse in Jeremiah 32, the response is revealing. It usually goes like this: I will say, "Is there anything too hard for God?"

People from the audience respond with a hearty chorus—"No!"

Then, I ask a second question. "Is there anything too hard for God to do…through *you*?"

Silence. A few grin, ducking their heads.

That is the way it is for all of us, isn't it? As long as we keep the principles of God's word at a nice, comfortable, theoretical distance, we can believe it all. It's only when it comes to putting it into practice that we become disbelieving. Somehow, God gets smaller when we get involved.

God is a great God, and He wants to be great through you.

When I began this book, I said that we would learn the keys to winning the whole world. As we give up all for Jesus, we will gain all. How does this work? First, you must recognize the greatness of God.

"In the beginning God…" is more than a good way to start off the first book of the Bible. It is literally true in every realm of existence. The only intelligent way to understand the complexities and vastness of the universe and life on our planet is to say, "In the beginning God…." All other theories stretch credibility far more than this simple statement from Genesis 1:1. God is the creator of everything and is still holding it all together by the word of His power (Hebrews 1:3).

Then, secondly, we need to look in the Bible and see what He is telling us to do and realize that it is possible. There is nothing too hard for God to do through us. He is good and just and would never give us impossible commands. It is possible for us to obey God. Anything is possible because, as we start to obey Him, He does what we cannot do. We do the possible and He does the impossible.

God has told us to take the world for Him. That's what it says in Matthew 28:18-20 when Jesus tells us that He has been given *all authority* in Heaven and on earth, all other issues and doubts are settled. Then He turns around and says to us, "Go therefore and *make disciples* of all the nations…teaching them to observe all that I commanded you…."

A tall order, isn't it? It's hard enough to disciple an individual, but here Jesus is commanding us to disciple nations!

Is your God big enough to do that through you?

How big is your God? Is He big enough to create Jesus without an earthly father? Many skeptics disbelieve the virgin birth because they can't imagine a God great enough to do that. But I believe not only did God once create a man without an earthly father—He created one without either a mother or a father! That man was Adam. He made Adam without either parent.

God created Adam and Eve, then told them He wanted them to multiply and take dominion over the earth (Genesis 1:28 KJV). Mankind has done well with the first part of that command: We have multiplied and replenished the earth with five billion of us. But the second part of God's purposes have been delayed.

They were delayed when Adam and Eve gave over the dominion of the earth to Satan in the Garden of Eden. The scriptures call the devil, "the god of this world" (2 Corinthians 4:4). How did he get that position? God didn't give it to him! Man did when he entered into conspiracy with Satan against God.

I find there are two extremes among Christians today. On one side, there are those who ignore the existence of the devil. They may even go as far as to say he doesn't exist at all, or that he is an analogy for the evil in the world. At the other extreme are Christians who attribute everything to Satan, giving him too much power.

We must avoid both extremes: We must understand who the enemy of God and our souls is and see how we can win over him.

In scriptures, such as Isaiah 14, Luke 10:18,19, Ezekiel 28 and others, we learn that Satan was a created being with lots of understanding and knowledge, who at one time stood in God's very presence. He chose to rebel against God, and one-third of the angels followed him in his rebellion (Daniel 8:10-11 and Revelation 12:4). He and this group were thrown out of Heaven, and sometime later (we aren't told how long) Satan again showed up in the Garden of Eden in the form of a serpent, tricking God's new creation into joining his rebellion.

When Adam and Eve sinned, they released Satan to become active in the world. He received his authority as prince of this world from them. And from the Garden of Eden until this moment, every time a person sins, Satan's ill-gotten authority on earth is increased a little more. When we sin, it's like we say to the devil, "…thy kingdom come, thy will be done on earth!"

Sin is the will of the devil and sinning helps to secure his throne.

With that background, let's look at Satan's weaknesses. He does have them. In fact, he has some serious problems. I like the way "Holy Hubert," a street preacher in Berkeley, California, put it. When confronting a ranting mob of radicals, bent on tearing him limb from limb, Holy Hubert waved his Bible and yelled, "I've read the end of the book, fellas, and *we win!*"

We must realize the devil is only a created being. Satan is not the opposite of God—he's not some evil, equal counterpart. God is all-powerful, all-knowing and everywhere present. Satan is none of the above.

It's almost funny how many of us forget that. I travel frequently. Sometimes I find myself on four continents in the space of a few weeks' time. Yet in each place, I hear Christians talking about this one individual—Satan—and how he has personally been after them that very week. But Satan can only be in one place at one time—he's not God!

And the devil cannot know your thoughts, either. In 1Kings 8:39 and Psalms 139, we learn that only God knows our hearts and thoughts completely.

Satan doesn't have all power. He has some magic tricks that he likes to show off to those who venture into the realm of the occult. But he doesn't have all power, like

God. God is the creator, and Satan can't create anything. He can only father lies.

Even man has been given power Satan hasn't. Man can multiply, but the devil can't even do that. He still has the same number of demons as he did when he led those one-third in rebellion against God and was cast out of Heaven.

But even if the devil had two-thirds of the angels and God had only one-third, he would still be outnumbered because of who God is! The Word of God declares the amazing fact that we have the advantage over Satan because Christ in us is greater than the devil (1 John 4:4).

Are you feeling a little taller yet? Jesus in you is greater than all the demonic hosts and all the evil that's in our world (Luke 10:19)! There is nothing that God cannot do through you if you are obedient and submissive to Him. If you have given over your rights, if you are standing barefoot in His presence, He is promising to give you all the land that the sole of your foot treads upon (Joshua 13).

When man fell into sin in the Garden, he didn't do away with God's purpose for him, which is to take authority and rule over the earth. He merely postponed it, because man lost his power to Satan. Jesus came to recapture that lost authority. He was born as a baby, lying in a dirty animal shelter. He took the role of a servant, giving up all His rights. He took the road of submission all His life, and taught us that the meek will inherit the earth. He showed us how to regain that authority we lost.

Jesus didn't take control of the earth through pride, like Satan tried to do when he rebelled against God. He didn't use threats or bribes, like Satan uses with man. He used the strategy of serving in love. "Follow me," He said. Take up your cross, die to your selfish desires. If you try to keep your life, you'll lose it. But if you lose your life for My sake and the gospel you will save it. What shall it profit a man if he gains the whole world and loses his own soul? (Mark 8:34-36).

On the surface, God's way seems foolish. How can we win by losing? But on the cross, Jesus, the Lamb, defeated Satan, the wolf, by dying. He went down to Hell and after three days, God raised Him up. He emerged the winner, leading a great group of hostages free with Him! Then God gave Him a name above every name, promising that someday every knee would bow and every tongue would confess that Jesus is Lord (Philippians 2:10).

God is already in the process of bringing every knee to bow. He's not waiting until the last battle and He doesn't want us to wait either. He is winning, one soul at a time, one cause, one nation, one people group. And He won't stop until His earth is again recaptured.

Does this mean we can have Utopia now? No. That will happen only when Jesus comes again. But we can extend Jesus' leadership now, in many lives and in many categories. It doesn't take equal parts of salt and water to make salty water. And we are the salt of the earth. We are also the light of the world. It's time to obey Isaiah 60:1 and rise up and let our light shine in this darkened generation.

Don Richardson, his wife and baby, went to live among the Sawi tribe in Irian Jaya to give them the gospel. This tribe were headhunters and cannibals, whose constant warfare was driving them near to extinction. Within a few years after the Richardsons arrived, a majority of the Sawis had become Christian. Not all of them—it wasn't suddenly a Paradise. Nor was it some kind of Christian dictatorship, for there were still sinners among the Sawis who chose not to worship God.

But the effect of the gospel has penetrated the entire Sawis society. Headhunting and cannibalism have stopped altogether. They have become leaders in commerce among other tribes in their area, with a variety of small business ventures. And the Sawis are also sending out missionaries to other people groups in the jungles of Irian Jaya. They have become the salt and the light in their part of the world.

If it can happen in an entire tribe, it can happen in an entire nation.

Jeremiah 27 promises an amazing thing. The Lord tells us first that He made the earth, the men and the animals that are on the earth by His great power. Then He says, "I will give it to the one who is pleasing in My sight."

God went on in this passage to say He was giving the land He had promised to Abraham's descendants to Nebuchadnezzar—a heathen king! Imagine how the Israelites felt when Jeremiah declared this. Cries of, "False prophet!" filled the air. They had read the scriptures. They knew that God had promised this land to Abraham, way back in Genesis 13. Yet, the Israelites held the Promised Land described by those boundaries only for a very brief time. Why?

The Israelites failed to hold onto the Promised Land because they didn't fulfill the second part of that covenant between God and Abraham. The first part promised, "I will make of you a great nation and I will bless you...." The second part declared that through the Israelites, all the people of the earth would be blessed (Genesis 12:2-3).

Like Christians today, the children of Israel liked the first part. They smiled: "God is going to bless me!" But they forgot the second part: "God wants to bless all the nations of the earth through me."

Since the beginning, God's purposes have not changed. He wanted Adam to take leadership over the earth. He wanted His chosen people to bless the whole earth. Through Christ, we have all become His chosen people (Romans 2:29), and He still wants the same thing for us that He wanted for Adam. He wants to bless us and through us, the entire world.

If you try to take only the first part of the covenant—even if you promise to pay tithes on the blessing—it is not enough. God will not continue to bless you unless you take on the second half, carrying His blessing to all the earth.

God promised in Jeremiah 27 to give the world to the one who pleased Him. Jesus pleased God completely, so God is giving the earth to Him. He declared, "This is my beloved Son with whom I am well pleased" (Matthew 3:17). That is the basis for Jesus saying, "All authority in heaven and on earth has been given to me" (Matthew 28:18). And that was the reason Jesus was able to turn and say to us, "As the Father has sent me, even so I send you" (John 20:21). He is including us in the process of reclaiming the land. Jesus is sending us into the world as missionaries, or sent ones. You can be a missionary to the business world, a missionary to the media, or you can be like Daniel—a missionary who ends up as prime minister.

There are five clear places in God's Word where He gives us the Great Commission. (Actually, there seem to be at least five hundred, but everyone agrees on these five as the most distinct.)

In Mark 16:15, we were given the **scope** of the Great Commission. We are to take the gospel to every person in our generation. I believe God gave that as a literal command to every generation since Christ. We founded Youth With A Mission on the belief that it can be done in our time.

We are given the **content** of the Great Commission in Luke 24:47. Repentance and forgiveness of sins are to be our message.

John 20:21, as we have noted, states that Jesus is the **sender**. Acts 1:8 tells us the **way** to do it: through the power of the Holy Spirit.

Lastly, the passage in Matthew 28:18-20 shows the **extent** of the Great Commission: We are not only to proclaim His Good News to every creature. We are to take the leadership God promised Adam in the Garden. All authority is given to Jesus and we are to disciple nations, teaching them to do everything Jesus has commanded us.

Some have trouble with this concept of Christian leadership. They say, "Hold on! Isn't this the end times? Aren't things supposed to get worse and worse until Jesus returns and cleans it all up? If we try to take ground for God in this world, maybe we are fighting against His purposes and the fulfillment of prophecies about the end of the world!"

A few years ago, some Christians in California became alarmed over the possible passage of a law condoning homosexual practices and extending moral wrongs as legal rights. They felt this law would be dangerous to society—especially to innocent youth and children. These Christians decided to try and rally other local believers to communicate their position to the authorities. They enlisted some support, but they were dismayed at the answer they received from many Christians. "Don't you know this is the end times? It's supposed to get more and more wicked, then Jesus will return." Their reaction implied that it was God's will for evil to triumph.

If we're not careful, we can use teaching on the end times as an excuse to do nothing. It can be a form of fatalism that says, "We can't act in politics, or in the media, or in any other significant arena of influence and leadership, because that would be working against God."

I don't claim to be an expert when it comes to end-times prophecies. Like any other Christian, I read my Bible and try to discern what is going on around me. But one thing I do believe very clearly: Jesus told us to *occupy* until He came (Luke 19:13 KJV). It isn't occupying the earth if we hole up in a religious enclave and let everything outside our church walls rot away.

I believe the Lord wants us to aggressively go out and reclaim lost territory from Satan and leave the timing and conclusion of history to Him. We're still making the same mistake Jesus was correcting in Acts 1:6,7, when the disciples were pressing Him to know if they were in the end times. Jesus replied, "It is not for you to know...." The timing of the end of this world is in the Father's hands.

Revelation 11:15 promises that someday the kingdoms of this world will all belong to Jesus. Right now, we should be advancing towards that goal. Luke 17:21 KJV explains that the kingdom of God is within us. Jesus Christ already rules in our hearts. When He rules in my life or in yours, He is already ruling in whatever area of influence we have in this world. Let's extend that realm of influence.

Satan knows all this and he must be worried. He can't create like God, or multiply like man. His present strategy is to try—through abortion, war, disease, strife and violence—to stop the multiplication of man. The devil is a destroyer. His purpose is to try and limit man. After all, he is losing his ratio. When he tempted Adam and Eve, there were only two human beings and he had one-third of the angels. Each week that the human race gets larger, Satan's ratio of demons to humans shrinks. So how does he maintain his control?

In some ways, Satan is smarter than we have been. He has targetted the most influential areas of human concern and has captured the few people in top leadership over those areas. Satan doesn't concern himself with the drunk, sitting on a sofa watching television through bleary eyes. He doesn't use him to try and rule the world. The devil goes for the leaders, using threats and bribes to control them and through them, the masses.

We have a number of YWAM missionaries working in Thailand. In that region, we learned about a warlord who operates just across the border in the area of Burma called the Golden Triangle. In this small, mountainous region, much of the world's heroin is grown. The whole endeavor is led by one man. This underworld king has one hundred loyal lieutenants. A huge cash-flow comes from all over the world to him in return for the heroin he supplies. The hundred from his inner circle go out and recruit other young men at gunpoint to join their forces. *Threat.* As they join the warlord's army, they are given pay, drugs and women. *Bribe.*

Through threat and bribe, this warlord exerts control over his one hundred lieutenants, over the thousands of young men hired to fight for him and, ultimately, over millions of drug addicts on the streets of New York, Amsterdam, London, Hong Kong, Sao Paulo and cities throughout the world.

This warlord, we learned, is himself a drug addict. He lives out his days in fear that he will be killed and replaced by another ambitious man. Satan is ruling over millions through this one man, who has become a slave himself.

Only one example, but it shows us how Satan uses his limited resources to hold onto his power as the god of this world. With his threats and bribes on a few in influential posts, he controls millions of people. But Jesus says, "Fear not." Perfect love casts out all fear. We can lead through love and win over the enemy.

In 1975, I was praying and thinking about how we could turn the world around for Jesus. A list came to my mind: seven areas. We were to focus on these categories to turn around nations to God. I wrote them down, and stuck the paper in my pocket:

1. **the home**
2. **the church**
3. **the schools**
4. **government and politics**
5. **the media**
6. **arts, entertainment and sports**
7. **commerce, science and technology**

The next day, I met with a dear brother, the leader of Campus Crusade For Christ, Dr. Bill Bright. He shared with me something God had given him—several areas to concentrate on to turn the nations back to God! They were the same areas, with different wording here and there, that were written on the page in my pocket. I took it out and showed Bill. Amazing coincidences like this happen all the time when Christians listen to the still, small voice of the Holy Spirit.

These seven spheres of influence will help us shape societies for Christ. God gave us these handles to use in carrying out Matthew 28 and discipling nations for Him. He obviously didn't just intend them for us in YWAM, or for those in Campus Crusade. I believe He is wanting all His people to see these seven and use them to extend Christ's reign throughout the earth.

How do we go about reclaiming these seven areas that are so influential in any nation?

First, we are to take territory from Satan in the place of prayer. With the power of the Holy Spirit, through the mighty weapons of spiritual warfare enumerated in Ephesians 6:10-20, 2 Corinthians 10:1-6 and James 4:7-10, we are told to pull down the devil's strongholds. We must pray against the enemy's influence in whatever area we are aware.

One person put it this way: Going with the gospel to every person (Mark 16:15) is like God's infantry. Discipling nations (Matthew 28:18-20) is His air force. And intercession for the nations (Daniel 9, Nehemiah 9, Ezra 9 and Colossians 3:1) is like intercontinental missiles. Praying is a very powerful part of the spiritual warfare we enter into to recapture this world for Jesus Christ.

Our prayers should be specific. As we listen to the voice of the Holy Spirit in our minds, He will tell us how to pray. (See Proverbs 3:5,6; Isaiah 55:8; Isaiah 59:16; 1 Timothy 2:1-6; Isaiah 62:6,7.) We then pray for the Holy Spirit to bring His influence to people in a strategic area— let's say it is regarding the government of a certain region. We should pray for a Christian witness to come to the individuals in that government, leading them towards the Lord Jesus. Then, if individuals won't submit to the Lord Jesus, we can pray that God will replace them, putting someone else in their place who will do His will.

This is what is implied every time we pray this phrase in the Lord's Prayer: "Thy kingdom come, thy will be done on earth as it is in Heaven." If His will were presently being done everywhere on earth, then it wouldn't be necessary for Jesus to tell us to pray that it would be!

After we have prayed for a specific category—be it a government, a school system, an area of the media, or whatever—God may then choose to use us in the very arena for which we have been praying. He may call us to penetrate that influential place for Him, placing us, like Daniel or Joseph, in a place of authority. In whatever area of influence God has given us, whether it's our family or a presidential palace, we are to live out His will in our lives. We aren't to do it in a way that lords it over others, but we are to be servants like Jesus was. Jesus wants to rule the world through us. But He extends His authority through us as He sees us giving up our rights for His sake and the gospel's (Mark 10:42-45).

Let's look at those seven areas again.

The Home

Through families, we are discipling the next generation of every nation on earth. Mothers and fathers are already discipling that next generation, for good or for bad. We can seek to establish Christian homes along biblical patterns that will be light even in places of gross spiritual darkness. I know of one family living in a country totally hostile to the gospel, working in a professional field. Because of strict laws against speaking on religious matters, they are greatly restricted in their witness. But they have reported that even the manner in which the husband relates to his wife and children is having an impact on the people around them. They are being drawn to the light of Jesus through the role model of this Christian family in their neighborhood.

The Church

Through churches, we are to disciple the nations of the world. How do we do this? I don't believe we are to do it by staying inside the walls of the church and believing it is Christ's Kingdom on earth. Attending church should be like a pit stop for Christians. The race is going on out in the world. The Kingdom of God is in us, and we take it out into the world wherever we go. We come to church again and again to get our tanks filled, to be fed, revived and restored, before going out again into the race to establish God's Kingdom in the world.

The Schools

From daycare centers and preschools, to graduate schools in the most prestigious universities of the world, the next generation is being influenced every day. This is a precious opportunity—an arena to shape the world for Jesus.

In Iceland during the ninth century, pagan Vikings came ashore and found a small population of Christians from Ireland. The Vikings made the Irish Christians their slaves and gave them what they considered a menial job—taking care of their children. The slaves taught the children and within three generations, they shaped a country. In the year 1,000, the people of Iceland voted to declare themselves a Christian nation.

Christians must be involved in every sphere of education: writing curriculum, teaching and administrating. Some should remain as salt and light in public schools while others lead in Christian schools. Parents are to be active, too, partnering with the teachers and delegating authority to the teachers to disciple their children.

The Media

Media-bashing has become a popular sport lately. Everyone from right to left in the political spectrum, as well as many Christians have become convinced that the media folks are conniving to rob them of their rights. But how many of us realize that this is a mission field of enormous proportions? According to a recent poll by Lichter and Rothman of 238 media elite, fifty percent claim to have no religious belief at all. Only three to five percent go to church or synagogue regularly.

This is a rate of unevangelized people equal to many so called "closed countries."

Pick your least favorite newsman. Get his or her face firmly in your mind. Then realize that this is a person for whom Jesus Christ hung on the cross—this is an individual worth the sacrifice of the Son of God.

It is hard to overstate the importance of the electronic and print media in shaping our society. Why then have Christians ignored this arena, leaving a vacuum for the unrighteous to fill? We can't complain of the lack of truth in the press if we are not willing to go among them, carrying the One who said He was the way, the truth and the life. Again, some will be led to penetrate the non-Christian media while others work in Christian networks and newspapers.

Government

Have you ever said, "Don't get involved in politics! It's a dirty business—no place for Christians?" If you have, you have been voicing the will of Satan. You didn't mean to, but you were giving the devil's point of view.

Where did we get the idea that Christians should not run for political office? We certainly didn't get it from the Bible. We don't even have to turn to the heads of state of Israel, like David or Solomon. After all, they were leading a country that at least gave lip service to being God's people. Look instead at two other examples—men who served in government in heathen countries—Daniel and Joseph.

These two young men exercised godly principles and conduct and found themselves as prime ministers. Early in their careers, no political pollster would have given them any chance of gaining their positions. Daniel was a refugee, a foreigner, an outsider who didn't play by the rules of his king's court. Joseph suffered sibling rivalry of the worst kind, met a woman who had a fatal attraction to him and found himself languishing in the dim recesses of an Egyptian dungeon. Not exactly the lifestyles of the rich and famous! Daniel, later in his political career, was thrown into a very small space where he was outnumbered by extremely large lions who hadn't had their lunch yet.

Can the godly win in the political arena? If it were possible in ancient Egypt and Babylon, it is possible today—in any country. But if a Christian seeks to serve the Lord in government, he or she will also have to face a modern den of lions. God will allow that to purge and build character, as well as to teach lessons that will later be applied in His style of leadership. Servant leadership. God is searching for men and women today who are willing to give up their rights and be raised to positions of national leadership. However, He will only exalt them after He has tested them to be sure they will not end up like King Saul—taken by the love of power, rather than remaining the servant of all.

Performing Arts, Entertainment & Sports

Whoa, you say. Surely this is the devil's own domain. Isn't *Christian entertainer* a contradiction in terms?

I don't know how I got this idea growing up, but somehow I became convinced that anything fun, anything exciting with movement and color was probably sinful.

Example: Really godly people dress plainly; the holiest wear all black (or all white, depending on the group).

Example: A good joke has no place among truly spiritual people.

Example: Anything is more sacred if it is done soberly, without any emotion. When at all possible, use seventeenth century language when you talk to God, like King

James English. Better yet, prayers should be said in a monotone, without any degree of inflection in the voice.

Perhaps you share only part of those ideas, but by and large, this is the picture we have painted to the world of what it means to be godly. And what does this say about God Himself? Since He is the most righteous of all, He must *never* smile! He must be dressed all in black, speak in a strange monotone, and never even move. (Didn't we learn to show respect for God as our parents constantly reminded us, "Sit still! You're in the house of God!")

No wonder the idea of a Christian entertainer strikes us as odd. Again, look at the scriptures. Do we see a dull God, a colorless God, a lifeless God? The devil wants us to think fun is his department, but that just isn't true. Read the book of Revelation and you'll see. There's a rainbow of color around God's throne, and the Creator of all energy is not sitting there impassively.

One of my favorite scriptures, in Zephaniah, shows God singing and rejoicing over us! He celebrates because of the actions of those who love Him. The God who created us in His image experiences emotions and knows great joy as well as sorrow. He is the center of excitement, the author of drama, pageantry, majesty and beauty.

Any territory which we abandon, Satan will fill. That has happened in the performing arts. Modern drama was born as a form of evangelism—the Church created morality plays to teach the truths of scripture to an illiterate public. We must recapture drama and every form of entertainment for Jesus, seeking Him for creative ways to show the world who He is.

Commerce, Science & Technology

Filthy lucre. Climbing up the ladder. The rat race. Even the common terms of our language show that we basically believe making money is a dirty business. Can a Christian succeed in business? Does the Holy Spirit want you to win in the corporate world? Can a rich man enter the Kingdom of Heaven?

Jesus said it wasn't easy. He knew how hard it was to serve God when we are blessed with material things. When the rich young ruler approached Him in Luke 18, Jesus looked into his heart and saw that money, not God, sat on the throne. He told him to give all that he had to the poor and follow Him.

Was Jesus giving a pattern for everyone? Yes, if money is number one it is an idol. The Lord will test you, to see if money means more to you than He does. He may ask you to give away everything you have, more than once. But it may be God's will for you to serve Him as a missionary in the business world, blessing you with finances so that you can be a blessing to many others. John Wesley, writing two hundred years ago, gave us up-to-date advice in his tract called, "The Use of Money." He urged those who loved Jesus to "Gain all you can…save all you can…and give all you can!" It's hard to improve on that advice.

Science and technology are also avenues for Christian service. These are categories which some Christians have avoided in the past. But true science and Bible Christianity are totally compatible. Not only that, science and technological desperately need the spiritual leadership of Christians. Never before has a society been able to work so many technological miracles, and yet been so unsure of its moral moorings. We need Christians who will enter these areas as their mission field.

When John Kennedy set the goal of putting a man on the moon before the end of the Sixties, his vision spun off into a knowledge explosion that we are still reaping the benefits of in everyday life. If the space race generated new devices, such as pocket calculators, lap top computers and other microelectronic wonders, *why couldn't the race to reach every creature with the gospel also expand new frontiers of knowledge?*

Let me give you just one example. At YWAM's Pacific and Asia Christian University, our provost is Dr. Howard Malmstadt, a brilliant scientist and a humble man of God. Under his direction in PACU's College of Science and Technology, our people have invented a compact chemical analyzer that can analyze everything from soil to blood serum. Its application in third world countries will include agriculture, industry, medicine and nutrition. Their next goal is to make a portable, battery-operated version of, the chemical analyzer, so that it can be taken on special missionary projects.

The heartbeat of the men and women at the College of Science and Technology is to help fulfill the Great Commission of Jesus Christ. At the same time, they're expanding fields of human knowledge.

Have you ever been asked by a full-time Christian worker what you do for a living and you've replied with a little shrug, "Oh, I have a secular job"? Immediately, the distinctions are drawn. Sacred and secular. Clergy and laymen. God's work, my work, the devil's work.

It works out like this in our minds. There is a kingdom of darkness—that takes place mostly on Friday and Saturday nights. The kingdom of light, God's Kingdom, happens on Sunday. The rest, Monday through Friday, is the secular kingdom. You don't think or talk about the other two kingdoms on workdays. You just do your job and get your paycheck.

This is not a Bible-based idea. I believe that for the Christian there is no such thing as the secular world. Every person is in one kingdom or the other: light or darkness.

We need to see this, then pray, "Thy kingdom come, Thy will be done in my job...in my business...in my career... in my farm...in my schoolroom...in my television station..." or in whatever area of influence and work to which God has called you.

We have been so split in our thinking as Christians that we have been confused and have confused the world watching us. There are only two kingdoms and they are at war. We need to win for the kingdom of light by moving into these seven areas of influence in the opposite way that Satan is working. Where he is spreading hate, we must show love. Where greed prevails we must outdo everyone in our giving, where intolerance is winning we need to show loyalty and forgiveness. God's Spirit enters into this world through His people, moving in the opposite spirit to wrestle the power from the god of this world and give it to Jesus, who is King of kings and Lord of lords.

Jesus has commanded us to go and disciple all nations. In the past we have gone into countries as missionaries, giving the gospel and teaching the people how to read and write. We didn't get involved in teaching government, politics or economics. We let the Marxists do that. In country after country in the Third World, the Communists took young men educated in missionary schools and "discipled" them on how to run a government.

But God is saying to us, "I know more about running a government than anyone. I know more about farming or fishing than you do. I know more about your business, your teaching. I know how to best communicate and use the media. I want to teach you My principles, so that you can teach others to observe all I have commanded and have a great harvest of souls. I have a calling for you and I want you to succeed at it. I just need for you to obey Me."

As we disciple the nations by giving them godly economic systems, Bible-based forms of government, education anchored in God's Word, families with Jesus at the head, entertainment that portrays God in His variety and excitement, media that is based on communicating the truth in love, and churches that serve as sending stations for missionaries into all areas of society, we will see the fulfillment of the Great Commission and multiplied millions coming into the Kingdom of God. Jesus promises that as we do this, "I am with you always, even to the end of the age" (Matthew 28:20).

Jesus has promised to give the earth to the meek, to the barefoot, to those who have surrendered their rights to Him. He wants us to claim the nations of the earth as His inheritance. He promises us that we will gain it all if we give it all.

It won't be easy. He doesn't promise comfort or ease. He promises His soldiers will have harder beds. Jesus said, "The foxes have holes, and the birds of the air have nests; but the Son of Man has nowhere to lay His head" (Matthew 8:20).

Jesus doesn't promise you will be rich; He promises to meet your needs. He will feed you, but the food might not always be what you like. He promises that you will have shelter, though it may be in crowded conditions. He promises that you may be arrested like He was arrested. You may even be one of the more than 300,000 who will die this year for the sake of getting the gospel out. But He also promises that you will reach an entire generation—every creature! For the promise is included in the commandment when He says, "I want you to go into all the world and preach the gospel to every creature."

He says to occupy until He comes. To occupy means to take leadership. It's not huddling together on some mountaintop wearing white robes, waiting for the end. When an occupation army moves into a nation they take authority in the economy, the military, the media and the schools. Jesus is telling us to take authority.

How do we do it? Not by force. We are to do it by becoming His slaves. It's the opposite way the world conquers. We are to take leadership through serving—as slaves, as the meek, as the humble. *The meek will inherit the earth.*

Does this sound impossible? Not at all. If you try to save your life, you'll lose it. But if you lose it for the Lord's sake and the gospel's, you will save it. Jesus did it. He humbled Himself as far down as anyone could possibly lower themselves. Right down to the bottom of Hell itself. Now God has exalted Jesus and promises that every knee will bow before Him. That same Jesus is telling us to follow Him. Take up His cross. Take your shoes off. Go barefoot. Become a slave. Lose your rights and you'll win the Kingdom. You'll rule and reign with Jesus.

You'll gain the whole world for Jesus.

Study Guide

General Discussion:

1. What has Loren Cunningham, the author, just given up as the story begins?
2. Describe the negative, life-shaking events that threaten Loren's future.
3. How did God act in this crisis?
4. What is the key to winning major battles with the forces of Satan?

Personal Application

1. What are the greatest things you have given up for Jesus Christ?
2. How has God allowed you to be tested, and how has He carried you through these times of testing?
3. How has the Lord intervened or rewarded someone you know through the giving up of some right or possession?

General Discussion

1. What are some things you always do barefoot? What are some things you never do barefoot?
2. What do Moses, Boaz's relative, David, and Jesus have in common in baring their feet?
3. How would you contrast going barefoot in Bible times with going barefoot today?
4. What are some rights that Jesus gave up during His life on earth?
5. What rights did He surrender at the end of His time on earth?
6. Besides restoring us to God, why did Christ suffer as our substitute? See Philippians 2:5-11.
7. If rights are God's good gifts to us, why should we think about giving them back?
8. What is the greatest privilege of all?

Personal Application:

1. If some of the most outstanding people in the Bible—Jesus, Moses, and David—went barefoot before God, how is God inviting you to "go barefoot"?
2. What is the fastest or easiest way to make you lose your temper or make your blood boil?
3. What is the real or supposed right that this emotional trigger is connected to?
4. How might this right be interfering with God's plan for your life?
5. Thoughtfully read 1 Corinthians 6:7: "The very fact that you have lawsuits among you means that you have been completely defeated already. Why not rather be wronged? Why not rather be cheated?" Offer your right to Jesus Christ and prepare for Him to help you through a head-on challenge this week.

General Discussion:

1. What are the two fundamental rights and cornerstones of human society?
2. Describe the relationship between "rights" and "responsibilities."
3. How should we understand Christ's words to "hate" one's closest family members and even one's own life? (Matthew 1:37; Luke 14:26)
4. Does God ask us to give up any rights that He has not given up?
5. What happened when Loren and his wife, Darlene, gave up their right to be together and their right to their children?
6. How did Loren's children feel about his absences after his prayer of relinquishment?

Personal Application:

1. Do you occasionally feel short-changed in regard to marriage or family? How?
2. Ask Christ to change your attitude from one of "sacrifice" to one of "privilege" in connection with an unfulfilled desire. Write a short prayer of thanksgiving for something positive God has done in this area of your life.
3. Loren and Darlene set up definite boundaries governing the length and frequency of their separations. As you follow God in a prayerful step or relinquishment, ask Him to show you what boundaries should guard your relationships.
4. When Jesus' mother and brothers came to see Him, Jesus looked at his followers and declared, "Here are my mother and brothers! Whoever does God's will is my brother and sister and mother." How does this relate to a sacrifice in your life?

General Discussion:

1. Is money a gift or a curse?
2. What are two Scriptures that point to a biblical right of ownership?
3. What was the most common topic in Jesus' preaching and teaching?
4. Describe why Loren thinks that poor people are more tempted by money than rich people are. What does he see as stronger temptations for the wealthy?

Personal Application:

1. How do you think the prophet Elijah felt as he asked a penniless, starving single mother for her last loaf of bread?
2. What does Jesus see in your checkbook? What is the pattern of your giving to Him and His work?
3. Which is your greatest temptation for "mis-giving": greed, giving to get; manipulation, giving to control; pride, giving for recognition; or guilt, giving to bail out God?
4. Loren identifies giving's proper motivation as giving "to obey and please our heavenly Father"— giving "out of a pure heart, obeying the promptings of the Holy Spirit." When have you seen God respond to Spirit-directed giving?
5. As stated in this chapter, "Those who are willing to give freely as the Lord leads will be allowed the privilege of seeing God multiply their resources to reach the world." What is in your pocket right now? Are you willing to let God tell you what to do with it? If you are, you are on the brink of a great adventure.

General Discussion:

1. A young person once asked General William Booth of the Salvation Army what to do with his life since he had never had a call from God. General Booth answered, "You mean you've never HEARD the call!" What did he mean?
2. When Brazilian missionary Braulia Riberio led a team of women to a new tribe in the Amazon rain forest, the first representatives they met wore red paint on their naked bodies and carried bows and arrows. They grabbed the workers, ripped off their clothes and began smearing them with the same red dye. What was the meaning of this aggressive action?
3. Giving up the right to being comfortable at home is difficult. Yet Loren asserts that working "with people who are not like you, who think (and believe) differently than you do...is even harder." What does he mean by this? See Ephesians 4:2-13.

Personal Application:

1. When you have traveled away from your home region or country, what things have stood out as strange? What things have you missed?
2. Braulia Riberio, the Brazilian missionary, initially misinterpreted the tribe members' actions. Think about a recent time when you may have misunderstood someone's words or actions toward you.
3. Loren believes that liberty is "servanthood to Christ's Great Commission and unity with others who are different." Who are some Christians you have separated yourself from, either in the past or now? Was this division pleasing or displeasing to Christ? Why?
4. One out of ten people on earth speaks English, yet nine out of ten sermons are in English, and nine out of ten dollars given for evangelism are spent in the United States. Ask the Lord to show you your part in correcting this imbalance.

General discussion:

1. How did these Bible characters give up the right to reputation: Noah (Genesis 6:14, 22), Mary (Matthew 1:18-19), Paul (Philippians 3:4-7)?
2. How did Jesus treat His rights to sleep (Luke 6:12) and food (Luke 4:1-2)?
3. Read Hebrews 11, the faith "hall of fame." What is the relationship between faith and God's deliverance?

Personal Application

1. How have you been misunderstood or rejected for following Christ?
2. Thinking about His own rejection, Jesus prophesied in John 15:18-21 about what kind of response we will face. Read this passage. How does it make you feel?
3. "God has said, 'Never will I leave you; never will I forsake you'" (Hebrews 13:5). Jesus promised, "Surely I am with you always, to the very end of the age" (Matthew 28:20). How do these promises relate to Jesus' prophecy in Question 2?

General Discussion

1. What, according to Loren, is God's healing agent?
2. How does Romans 5:8 relate to forgiveness as a choice rather than as something that happens when it feels right?
3. Describe how these seven problems get in the way of forgiveness: (1) not choosing (2) failure to forgive yourself (3) jealousy (4) pride (5) not understanding God's character—His mercy (6) double standard (7) fear.
4. How does false humility hide pride?

Personal Application

1. Jesus said, "If you forgive men when they sin against you, your heavenly Father will also forgive you. But if you do not forgive men their sins, your Father will not forgive your sins" (Matthew 6:14-15). These have been called the scariest words in the Bible. What comes to mind when you read these verses?
2. When Enrico helped thieves steal his lumber, they came to know Jesus. When he visited his ex-commandant to offer him a meal, the Nazi knelt and asked Jesus to save him. Loren writes that in his forgiveness toward these men Enrico was like Jesus on the cross, extending forgiveness to us before we repented. Who is Jesus asking you to forgive—before that person repents?
3. Pray the Lord's Prayer. Repeat the phrases of the forgiveness petition, saying, "Forgive me my trespasses/debts as I forgive _________ who ___________ against me." (Fill in the blanks with the name of the person who wronged you and what that person did to you.)

General Discussion

1. If Jesus was meek when He took out a whip and chased the moneychangers from the temple, what is meekness?
2. "A gentle answer turns away wrath" (Proverbs 13:22). How does this proverb illustrate the principle of moving in the opposite spirit to the forces of darkness?
3. Describe three reasons God allows Satan's attacks.
4. How does Proverbs 13:22 relate to the enemy's attacks against us?
5. When Loren bid on a hotel for ministry in Hawaii, he sensed the enemy attacking through a spirit of greed. What did he and hundreds of his team members do to fight back?
6. What are six other spirits against us, besides the spirit of greed?

Personal Application

1. In Ephesians 4:15, Paul urges Christians to speak the truth in love. How is this a part of acting meek?
2. Since pride is trying to be known for something that you are not, both boasting and covering up stem from pride. Describe a time you concealed something out of pride.
3. Loren lists seven attitudes and their corresponding spirits. Which one is hindering you the most at this time?
4. How could you move in the opposite way to win with God?

General Discussion

1. Who made Satan "the god of this world"?
2. When we sin, whose will are we following?
3. According to Matthew 5:5, what is one prize Jesus promises those who are meek?
4. Who does God have in mind besides ourselves when He blesses us with Christ?

Personal Application

1. Society can be divided into these seven areas: (1) home (2) church (3) schools (4) government policy (5) media (6) arts, entertainment, sports (7) commerce, science, and technology. In which areas do you think God wants you to focus your efforts?
2. Loren tells us, "First we are to take territory from Satan in the place of prayer." What should you pray for to move forward in your focus area from Question 1?
3. "Gain all you can. Save all you can. Give all you can," John Wesley urged Christians. Which are you doing the best? Which area needs the most improvement?
4. Is there anything too hard for God to do…through you?

Other Recommended Books from YWAM Publishing

WHY NOT WOMEN?
A Fresh Look at Scripture on Women in Missions, Ministry, and Leadership

by Loren Cunningham and David Joel Hamilton, $14.99

Why Not Women? brings light, not just more heat, to the church's crucial debate with a detailed study of women in Scripture; historical and current global perspectives; an examination of the fruit of women in public ministry; and a hard-hitting revelation of what's at stake for women, men, the Body of Christ, God's Kingdom, and the unreached. (ISBN 1-57658-183-7)

IS THAT REALLY YOU, GOD?
Hearing the Voice of God

by Loren Cunningham, $9.99

This practical guide to hearing God's voice shows how an ordinary man who was committed to hearing God and obeying Him became the founder of the largest interdenominational missions organization in the world. (ISBN 0-927545-22-5)

DARING TO LIVE ON THE EDGE
The Adventure of Faith and Finances

by Loren Cunningham, $9.99

Living by faith is not the domain of only those Christians called to "full-time" ministry. What is important is not our vocation, but whether we are committed to obeying God's will in our lives. If we are willing to step out in faith, doing whatever God has asked us to do, we will see His provision. A Christian who has experienced this is spoiled for the ordinary. (ISBN 0-927545-06-3)

FOLLOWING JESUS
Attaining the High Purposes of Discipleship

by Ross Tooley, $9.99

Following Jesus brings vision and direction to Christians who want to know God and make Him known. With straightforward teaching drawn from true stories of God's faithfulness and guidance, Ross Tooley examines how our passionate and patient God leads His present-day disciples into the dreams He has for them and for His Kingdom. (ISBN 1-57658-205-1)

SPIRITUAL WARFARE FOR EVERY CHRISTIAN
How to Live in Victory and Retake the Land

by Dean Sherman, $12.99

God has called Christians to overcome the world and drive back the forces of evil and darkness at work within it. Spiritual warfare isn't just casting out demons; it's Spirit-controlled thinking and attitudes. Dean delivers a no-nonsense, both-feet-planted-on-the-ground approach to the unseen world. Includes study guide.
(ISBN 0-927545-05-5)

LOVE, SEX, AND RELATIONSHIPS

by Dean Sherman, $12.99

With clarity and a sharp wit, Dean Sherman illuminates the confusing and mysterious world of love, sex, and relationships in this accessible, hard-hitting examination of romantic love and sexuality in the Christian's life. Includes study guide. (ISBN 1-57658-141-1)

LEARNING TO LOVE PEOPLE YOU DON'T LIKE
How to Develop Love and Unity in Every Relationship

by Floyd McClung, $8.99

Does God really expect us to get along with each other? Floyd McClung offers challenging and practical answers for achieving productive, lasting relationships. Here is a firsthand account of how anyone can live in love and unity with others, both in the church and in the world. Includes study guide. (ISBN 0-927545-19-5)

INTERCESSION, THRILLING AND FULFILLING

by Joy Dawson, $11.99

This book proves that we are surrounded by opportunities to impact our world through the powerful means of intercessory prayer. *Intercession, Thrilling and Fulfilling* spells out the price of obedience but leaves us in no doubt that the rewards and fulfillment far outweigh that price. We become history shapers and closer friends of Almighty God. (ISBN 1-57658-006-7)

COURAGEOUS LEADERS
Transforming Their World

by James Halcomb, David Hamilton, and Howard Malmstadt, $15.99

Our world needs courageous leaders who will recognize the need for

God-motivated action and follow through with a God-led plan. Whether your vision for change is local or global, simple or complex, for home, business, or ministry, *Courageous Leaders* will help you remain on a true course and reach the goal set before you. (ISBN 1-57658-171-3)

THE LEADERSHIP PARADOX
A Challenge to Servant Leadership in a Power Hungry World

by Denny Gunderson, $9.99

What is the key to effective leadership? The ability to organize and take charge? The ability to preach and teach? Entrepreneurial skill? A charismatic personality? According to Jesus, none of the above. This refreshingly candid book draws us to the Master's side. Through the eyes of people who experienced Jesus firsthand, we discover insights that will challenge us to re-think our leadership stereotypes. Includes study guide. (ISBN 0-927545-87-X)

DISCIPLING NATIONS
The Power of Truth to Transform Cultures, 2nd Edition

by Darrow Miller, $14.99

The power of the gospel to transform individual lives has been clearly evident throughout New Testament history. But what of the darkness and poverty that enslave entire cultures? In *Discipling Nations,* Darrow Miller builds a powerful and convincing thesis that God's truth not only breaks the spiritual bonds of sin and death but can free whole societies from deception and poverty. Excellent study of worldviews. Includes study guide. (ISBN 1-57658-015-6)

INTERNATIONAL ADVENTURES
Amazing True Stories of Spiritual Victory and Personal Triumph

by various authors, $11.99 each

On every continent, in every nation, God is at work in and through the lives of believers. From the streets of Amsterdam to remote Pacific islands to the jungles of Ecuador and beyond, each international adventure that emerges is a dramatic episode that could be directed only by the hand of God...

Adventures in Naked Faith • ISBN 0-927545-90-X
Against All Odds • ISBN 0-927545-44-6
Dayuma: Life Under Waorani Spears • ISBN 0-927545-91-8

Imprisoned in Iran • ISBN 1-57658-180-2
Living on the Devil's Doorstep • ISBN 0-927545-45-4
The Man with the Bird on His Head • ISBN 1-57658-005-9
Tomorrow You Die • ISBN 0-927545-92-6
Torches of Joy • ISBN 0-927545-43-8
Totally Surrounded • ISBN 1-57658-165-9

CHRISTIAN HEROES: THEN AND NOW
Great missionary biographies!

by Janet and Geoff Benge, $6.99 each

This popular series chronicles the exciting, challenging, and deeply touching true stories of ordinary men and women whose trust in God accomplished extraordinary exploits for His kingdom and glory. Real people—incredible, inspiring true stories for ages 10 and up.

Gladys Aylward • ISBN 1-57658-019-9
Corrie ten Boom • ISBN 1-57658-136-5
William Booth • ISBN 1-57658-258-2
William Carey • ISBN 1-57658-147-0
Amy Carmichael • ISBN 1-57658-018-0
Loren Cunningham • ISBN 1-57658-199-3
Jim Elliot • ISBN 1-57658-146-2
Jonathan Goforth • ISBN 1-57658-174-8
Betty Greene • ISBN 1-57658-152-7
Adoniram Judson • ISBN 1-57658-161-6
Eric Liddell • ISBN 1-57658-137-3
David Livingstone • ISBN 1-57658-153-5
Lottie Moon • ISBN 1-57658-188-8
George Müller • ISBN 1-57658-145-4
Nate Saint • ISBN 1-57658-017-2
Mary Slessor • ISBN 1-57658-148-9
Hudson Taylor • ISBN 1-57658-016-4
Cameron Townsend • ISBN 1-57658-164-0
John Williams • ISBN 1-57658-256-6